"Out of all of the things that God could have given to us as an inheritance, He gave to us something and someone that is supernatural. The Spirit! In this book Venner Alston gives us not only a revelation of the supernatural but also guidance for how to walk in the manifestation of the supernatural in our lives. Get ready for a God encounter!"

Isaac Pitre, II Kings Global Network; founder,
Christ Nations Church; isaacpitre.org

"Dr. Alston issues a timely invitation for you to ascend through the Revelation 4 door to hear, see, and decree what the future holds. Use these Kingdom keys to open the gates and portals to your mind to stoke the fire on the altar of your heart as you enjoy her profound writings."

Dr. Barbie L. Breathitt, president, Breath
of the Spirit Ministries Inc.

"Life in the supernatural is an exciting life! Supernatural encounters can also be confusing or even fearful. This book brings clarity out of confusion. Venner Alston reveals wisdom that overpowers evil supernatural encounters. Every God-seeker should read and apply the principles found in this book."

Barbara Wentroble, president, International
Breakthrough Ministries; speaker and author

Encountering
the
LIVING
GOD

Books by Venner J. Alston

Encountering the Living God
Next-Level Believers
Next-Level Spiritual Warfare

Encountering
the
LIVING
GOD

UNLOCKING
THE SUPERNATURAL REALM OF HEAVEN

VENNER J. ALSTON

Chosen
a division of Baker Publishing Group
Minneapolis, Minnesota

© 2023 by Venner J. Alston

Published by Chosen Books
Minneapolis, Minnesota
www.chosenbooks.com

Chosen Books is a division of
Baker Publishing Group, Grand Rapids, Michigan

Printed in the United States of America

ISBN 978-0-8007-6306-0 (paper)
ISBN 978-0-8007-6335-0 (casebound)
ISBN 978-1-4934-4094-8 (ebook)

Library of Congress Cataloging-in-Publication Control Number: 2023022517

23 24 25 26 27 28 29   7 6 5 4 3 2 1

I dedicate this book to the watchmen and intercessors
who prayed and encouraged me through the writing of it.
Your prayers helped me access the necessary revelation
to bring understanding of God-encounters
to those who will read this book. Thank you.
I pray that you will continue to live
in the realm of encounters.

Contents

Foreword

I had my first encounter with God as a young child, and it changed my life. I had recently had a friend, a young boy in my neighborhood, get very sick and die. I was not yet a believer in Christ and did not know what to do with all the grief and emotions I was experiencing. I didn't understand death and was filled with fear about the future.

However, in the 1960s there was a program on television called *The Flying Nun*, starring Sally Field. She played a young nun who always got into trouble (and at some point in each show, strangely, she flew). But there was always a part when she would go into the church, get on her knees, fold her hands, look up to Christ on the cross, and tell Him her troubles. Miraculously, He would always help her out of her problems.

That was my only point of reference for prayer. So I went into my room, got on my knees by my bed, folded my hands, looked up to the ceiling, and told God all I was feeling.

Suddenly, I felt warm all over, as if someone had draped a warm blanket around my shoulders and put his arms around me. I sat there, feeling warm and loved, for some time. When I got up I felt better. The sorrow was gone. The heaviness was lifted. I was changed.

I didn't understand this at all. I had no knowledge of spiritual things. But I knew how good this encounter felt, so each night I would sneak away to my room to talk to God, and His arms would come around me each time in comforting presence.

This continued for nine years before I fully understood salvation, was able to hear the Gospel, and received Christ as my Savior. Encounters with God marked my life from my earliest days.

I have also had dark encounters with the devil or one of his demons. Shortly after my initial encounters with the Lord as a child, the enemy would manifest to me in my room and leave me in terror. Even after becoming a believer, I could discern demonic beings present in a room but had no idea what to do about it. On occasion, even now, the Lord will pull back the veil in the spirit and show me demonic beings, strongholds, and principalities so that I might take authority over them and expose their schemes.

I have not been a stranger to the supernatural realm, but have experienced both the sacred and the dark. God has invited each of us to see into the unseen realm and be empowered to bring transformation. John the Revelator experienced such an encounter when he said,

> Then suddenly, after I wrote down these messages, I saw a portal open into the heavenly realm, and the same trumpet-voice I heard speaking with me at the beginning said, "Ascend into this realm! I want to reveal to you what must happen after this." Instantly I was taken into the spirit realm.
>
> Revelation 4:1–2 TPT

God is still inviting us into the supernatural realm today. Since I became a believer, God-encounters continue to change and challenge me. I have experienced the overwhelming presence of the Lord in times of prayer and worship. When reading the Word and studying, I have sensed His Holy Spirit fill the room with that same weightiness of His glory from my childhood. I have experienced Him through hearing His voice, at times audibly, in my heart. Each word changed the course and direction of my life. I have encountered Him in dreams and visions, each one a supernatural experience that has brought revelation, direction, insight, and just the sheer joy of being with Him.

One encounter with the Living God will change everything.

It's for this reason I am so honored to introduce and recommend this book to you. Personal divine encounters have deeply transformed the life of the author, Venner Alston. She longs to see others experience the same richness of the glory and presence of God in their lives. She establishes a biblical understanding regarding divine encounters, but goes beyond this to invite us to see Him, know Him, and encounter Him as never before. You will find it is a vital and necessary part of the spirit life of every believer. You will sense the presence of the Living God and His abiding glory even as you read. Enjoy!

Jane Hamon, author, *Dreams and Visions*, *The Cyrus Decree*, *The Deborah Company*, *Discernment*, and *Declarations for Breakthrough*

Introduction

The Invitation

We were designed to operate in the supernatural realm. Out of everything God created, nothing is as unique as humankind. We are created in the image and likeness of God, who is the Supreme Ruler of the universe. Every aspect of our design reflects the intentionality of God in creating us with the capacity to operate in His realm, the supernatural.

Human beings, created in the image and likeness of God, are endowed with glory and honor:

> What is man that You are mindful of him, and the son of man that You attend to him?
>
> For You have made him a little lower than the angels, and crowned him with glory and honor. You have given him dominion over the works of Your hands; You have put all things under his feet.
>
> Psalm 8:4–6

The fact that we are made in God's image and likeness validates the truth that we are each capable of experiencing God beyond the temporal plane in amazing ways. Why was such an honor bestowed upon humankind? The answer: God designed us for fellowship with Himself. Our entire design is wired to sense knowledge of Him.

Sensing knowledge of God is the capacity to discern God around us. We see Him in creation when we look at the stars or feel the wind blowing. When we stand on the shore of a lake, a river, or an ocean, watching the waves roll back and forth yet not flow beyond their boundary, we are reminded of the powerful God of creation, who established boundaries for the waters, set the stars in place, and created the winds that blow. During these moments, we sense His presence in amazing ways.

However, there is a realm beyond "basic sense" knowledge. This realm is called "the realm of encounters." This is where the invitation is extended. It is where time suspends, and we are granted access to the eternal realm. This realm is where we have been seated in heavenly places with Christ (see Ephesians 2:6). Beyond sense knowledge, one of the purposes of God-encounters is that they are a pathway to revelation knowledge. They are a pathway to the glory realm of heaven. Our bodies can be healed, and yokes of bondage can be destroyed in this realm. Encounters provide an opportunity for you to know God in a deeper way. In encounters with God, we gain understanding of who we are in Him and His purpose for creating us. We are invited to "come in" and commune with the One who created us for Himself.

> **In encounters with God, we gain understanding of who we are in Him and His purpose for creating us.**

As believers, we are citizens of the Kingdom of God, created for the purposes of God. We are the Ekklesia, the "called-out ones" in New Testament Greek, and as such, we have been granted supernatural access into the realm of heaven. Understanding this truth is vital for our success and effectiveness in advancing God's Kingdom mandate. Jesus completed His earthly assignment and delegated authority to the Church (see Matthew 28:19–20; Mark 16:15–18). This means we have been commissioned to preach the Gospel message of the Kingdom, heal the sick, and cast out demons. This is the Church's mandate. Understanding this is vital to the advancement of the Kingdom. Weekly gatherings are for the purpose of strategic deployment into the places we have been assigned. Whether your assigned place is in the Church, business, education, marriage and family, arts and entertainment, media, or government, you were created for impact.

Encounters with the Living God who created and sent you are vital to the successful accomplishment of your mission. Jesus understood this truth. Throughout His ministry, Jesus referred to His relationship and communion with the Father (see John 14:6–21). Statements like the ones He made should form the basis of our understanding of God-encounters. Let me state that such encounters are not for the sake of having a supernatural experience. God has an agenda. He desires that we would know Him deeply and that from this place of deeply knowing Him, we would reveal Him through our lives, to the extent that men and women would desire Him. That's impact, and that's a key reason for the invitation!

I want to share with you a prophecy about your Kingdom authority. (In fact, from time to time throughout this book I'll share such prophetic words, whenever the Holy Spirit speaks something to my heart for you to hear, and I'll also talk more about the prophetic in chapter 3.) I heard the Spirit of God say this: *I am raising up disrupters. Those who understand their Kingdom authority. These holy ones move in My supernatural power. They are living portals through which My glory can be released. Through these disrupters, I will reveal My glory and display My power. Through these disrupters, there will be a great harvest of souls.*

These holy ones understand the necessity of supernatural encounters with the Living God, and they commit themselves to stepping into this realm to commune with Him. There are different types of encounters we may have when we do this. We can encounter God in our everyday, walking-around lives. Our first encounter is when we meet Jesus, our Redeemer. Encounters are moments when the realm of heaven opens, and we step in. I believe some moments might be in the form of God's whisper, and others might be God's voice as thunder. Both are encounters.

Encounters are moments when the realm of heaven opens, and we step in.

Another way to see encounters is as time interruptions. Not the nuisance interruptions we all experience, but moments when time suspends, and we access the timeless realm of the supernatural. I believe this is the realm where Adam and Eve lived in the Garden. We can see these moments as God came down in the cool of the day to commune with them (see Genesis 3:8). Adam and Eve encountered God in their everyday, walking-around lives, and so can you.

Maybe you are wondering why you need to read a book on the subject of encounters. Perhaps you are thinking that these kinds of experiences are only for the "super spiritual." I believe we are living in appointed times. God desires to reveal Himself and His plans to every generation. Every generation is invited to step into the realm beyond what our natural senses perceive. In reality, when we step into this realm beyond our natural senses, we are returning to the original paradigm of the Garden, where Adam was assigned. Encounters have meaning and purpose. They are news flashes from heaven. Something we have been praying and believing for manifests. As we occupy these incredible moments, everything seems to stop.

Yet it is important to understand that encounters are not the goal. This book is not designed to give you a formula, but to provide principles and keys to help you understand the pattern that governs God-encounters. Knowing God in a deeper way is the whole purpose of such encounters. Our knowing Him in a deeper way creates a sense of urgency and a desire in us to fulfill the will of heaven, including revealing Him on the earth. This is God's goal.

Encounters are experiences that bring reality and conviction to us. Unlike the birds, fish, and beasts of the field, we were created with the capacity to commune with God. He is inviting us to come away with Him so that He might share information that will raise our perspective to a higher level. He is longing for us to know Him. He wants us to experience Him at the deepest possible levels, and in so doing, we begin living in our original design, which is supernatural. It is from this vantage point that we can then fully "re-present" Him on the earth.

I wrote this book to help us understand that supernatural encounters with the realm of heaven are not only possible, but they are also necessary. I want you to know how much God desires for you to become comfortable with moving beyond natural sense knowledge of Him, to experiencing Him beyond the earthly domain through your spiritual senses.

Encounters are possible for everyone. Within these pages, you will discover why God invites humans from generation to generation to step beyond the earthly realm into the supernatural realm, which is eternal. What does God desire to accomplish by inviting us to encounter Him? He wants us to know Him! And to know that Satan is a counterfeit. Whatever God is doing, Satan attempts to create an imitation. This book will also discuss legal and illegal access into the supernatural realm. The apostle Paul admonished the Church not to be ignorant of the tactics of the enemy (see 2 Corinthians 2:11).

Many believers wrongly believe that encounters are only for the more spiritual believers, and they therefore don't exercise their faith to believe for these supernatural moments. Yet God desires that we all will encounter Him and "know" Him more deeply. Encounters confirm the reality of God to us. They give us an assurance that He is involved in the affairs of the earth. Encounters are immensely prophetic, as these moments "pull back" the curtain of heaven and reveal things we did not know.

> Encounters are immensely prophetic, as these moments "pull back" the curtain of heaven and reveal things we did not know.

At the end of each chapter ahead, you will find a "Prayer Activation" to help you not only understand the supernatural nature of encounters, but also activate your faith to go through the door into God's presence. It is my hope that this book will be the catalyst to the beginning of a new journey with you and God. My desire within these pages is to present God's manifesto. A *manifesto* is defined as "a statement in which someone makes his or her intentions or views easy for people to ascertain."[1] God desires us to encounter Him daily, regularly. Encounters must become a way of life for all of us, not an occasional occurrence in the life of a few. This book is an open expression of

God's invitation. Revelation 3:20 (VOICE) states, "Now pay attention; I am standing at the door and knocking. If any of you hear My voice and open the door, then I will come in to visit with you and to share a meal at your table, and you will be with Me."

The invitation has been given. How will you respond? May you enter through the door of encounters often! I pray that you will not be an infrequent visitor, but that you will live in the glory that abides in the place of God-encounters. As you do, your life will be transformed in amazing ways. Let's begin.

ONE

Understanding Encounters

> The secret things belong to the LORD our God, but those things which are revealed belong to us and to our children forever, so that we may keep all the words of this law.
>
> Deuteronomy 29:29

It was time for bed. It had been a long day, and I was ready to sleep. Shortly after lying down, I heard a sound over my shoulder that startled me. My husband had been scheduled to work third shift, and I was a new bride who was home alone. Hearing the sound, my first thought was that someone else was in the house. Somewhat apprehensive, I raised my head and looked around to see if I could locate the source of the sound.

What I saw was a golden globe at the top of the doorway. The shades of gold were not like anything I had ever seen. At one point the object became translucent, allowing me to see through it. I could hear a melodic sound coming from the beautiful golden globe at the top of the door. As suddenly as this strange but wonderful manifestation occurred,

I could see it dissipating, leaving me to wonder about this phenomenon. *What was it?* I wondered. *Where did it come from? Why was I seeing it?*

What Are Encounters?

A God-encounter is a face-to-face meeting during which there is a supernatural manifestation of God's presence in your life. What I mean by the term *face-to-face* is that God initiates a supernatural occurrence during which there is a manifestation of His presence in some way. These moments in time are often sudden, and we experience them in varying ways. Such ways can be (but are not limited to) dreams, open visions, and the appearance of angels or other auditory or visual representations God might choose to use to convey His message to us in that moment. As I said earlier, encounters are supernatural moments in time when the realm of heaven opens up. In these moments, we shift from the earthly domain into the supernatural realm of heaven.

Another way to understand this is that in those moments, we occupy two spheres—the heavenly and the earthly domains. We are alive on earth, yet during a God-encounter we also occupy the eternal realm of heaven. During some encounters, we are literally overtaken by the glory of God's presence. The weightiness, the *kābôḏ* of God,[1] comes upon us in such way that many of us fall under the power of His presence (see Exodus 16:7, 10; 24:16–17; Numbers 14:10, 21; 2 Chronicles 5:14; Isaiah 6:3). In other cases, an angelic messenger sent from God may appear. Throughout this book, we will discuss different encounter manifestations that may occur.

It is important, however, for you to understand that this book is not intended to create an encounter doctrine. In the absence of sound biblical understanding, Satan can infiltrate the Body of Christ with false teachings based on ignorance of the Word of God. The apostle Paul wrote about this problem to the Corinthian Church:

> But I fear that somehow, as the serpent deceived Eve through his trickery, so your minds might be led astray from the simplicity that is in Christ. For if he who comes preaches another Jesus, whom we have not preached, or if you receive another spirit, which you have not received, or another gospel, which you have not accepted, you might submit to it readily enough.
>
> 2 Corinthians 11:3–4

False doctrines were problematic in the early Church, and Paul found it necessary to instruct its members concerning being vigilant against them.

The Bible, which is the *Logos*, must be the first and final perspective we embrace for our lives. Understanding that God is a God of patterns and processes provides safeguards to protect us from error. Any revelation that violates the patterns and processes of God must be discarded quickly. It is vitally important for believers to guard their lives carefully from flaky opinions and teachings that violate the patterns of God and the rule of Scripture.

In the aftermath of some encounters with God, it is not unusual to lack the ability to articulate what has happened. In a later chapter, we will discuss this fact in more detail. For now, I want to convey the challenges of explaining these moments to other people who have not been privy to your experience. Even in a corporate gathering where the majestic presence of Jesus, the King of all kings, fills the room, some will fall under the weighty presence of God, while others might not. I have been asked about encounters I have experienced in our corporate gatherings and have sometimes lacked the ability to explain what happened. It was an overwhelming challenge for me to respond to simple questions such as, "Where did God take you?" "What did you see?" "What happened?" I believe this was due not only to the enormity of such experiences, but also because at the time, these types of experiences were new to me. I had yet to understand the language that would describe supernatural encounters from a personal perspective.

I caution you against creating a supernatural encounters pattern. Don't violate the pattern of Scripture. Every encounter must submit to Scripture. You cannot take your experiences and attempt to make them the rule for others. While there are similarities, every encounter is as different as the person who experiences God in this way. Some individuals have experienced supernatural encounters and were immediately able to fully describe their experiences. I was not one of them. I will say again, avoid creating an encounters doctrine, which can result in sensationalism and error. Encounters are not a doctrine. Doctrines must submit to Scripture, and interpretation must come from Scripture. Individual encounters are designed by God to increase our influence and effectiveness. God-encounters validate Scripture, and Scripture validates God-encounters.

> While there are similarities, every encounter is as different as the person who experiences God in this way.

Interpreting Encounters

Like dreams, encounters must be interpreted. Let's look again at the golden globe encounter I described to you. In her book *A to Z Dream Symbology Dictionary*, Dr. Barbie Breathitt writes, "To see a globe indicates that your life is balanced and in order so that you have an ability or calling to change the world. Step back and look again to gain a wider world view or heavenly perspective."[2] In that moment when I saw the globe, God was speaking to me about my life. He was giving me a small snapshot, which required interpretation, of His plans for me. He wanted me to know that I had been created for impact, not obscurity. At this point in my life, I was unaware of God's plans for me. God was encouraging me to gain His perspective for my future.

If you lack understanding of supernatural encounters, you can miss the message God is trying to convey to you. A simple example of this point can be found in lip reading. On occasion, I have tried to convey a message to someone without the use of audible or written language. I would simply get the person's attention and mouth the words. While some can receive a message this way, others cannot. They find it difficult to watch someone mouthing words and interpret what the person means. A factor creating this problem could be distance. If the distance between the person I'm attempting to communicate with and myself is too great, the message cannot be understood. The issue of distance can be problematic in interpreting encounter moments, too. This is a picture of living on a low spiritual plane. When your prayer life is shallow and inconsistent, it results in spiritual dullness. In other words, you lack sensitivity to spiritual things. When prayerlessness is a factor, you become unfamiliar with the way God speaks. In the same way that a child learns the voice of his or her parent through hearing the sounds and communications of the parent, we learn God's voice as He speaks to us during our times of prayer and communing with Him.

A second factor in interpreting encounters can be a lack of biblical reference points. All encounters can and should be interpreted through God's Word, the Bible. When you lack biblical understanding, you can misinterpret what God is saying to you. You can also miss the fact that God is speaking to you altogether. Let me say again, encounters are not for the benefit of our ego, wherein we create a mindset of overspiritualization. You must resist the spirit of pride, which can create a false perception that you are more spiritual than other people. God's purpose for encounters is to reveal His nature and character to us. Encounters strengthen our conviction and increase our faith.

The Supernatural Nature of Encounters

Let's look at the substance of supernatural encounters with God. First, the primary aspect of an encounter is that it is supernatural. Heaven invades earth. The domain that belongs to God invades the domain where we reside. In other words, earth meets heaven. The natural, temporal domain encounters the heavenly, eternal domain. God's intent might be revelational, restorative, reconciliatory, or judgmental between the individual(s) and Himself.

Second, an encounter occurs when God sovereignly convenes a meeting with us. Encounters with God are recurrent throughout Scripture. God met with Adam in the Garden (see Genesis 3:8–10). The murder of Abel by his brother Cain gives us a picture of encounters with a theme of judgment (see Genesis 4:4–15). Abram encounters the Living God, who established a covenant with him (see Genesis 13:14–17).

Although God initiates many encounters, I have had the opportunity to speak to individuals who have requested a meeting with Him. Several years ago, an amazing prophetic intercessor I know shared her testimony concerning her request to meet with God. She had gone through several major crises in her life, which had overwhelmed her. Thinking about her testimony now, I think she must have felt a bit like Job. She had experienced the loss of her daughter and then her husband. She was at a loss to understand the chain of events that had occurred in her life, and she decided to request a meeting with God. She prepared her questions and waited. After a period of time, God spoke to her and said, *I will meet with you today*. This was an encounter.

Third, although we often hear the term *encounter* used among those who identify as charismatic or Pentecostal, encounters are not limited to certain denominations. God invites everyone to draw near to Him, with the promise that when we do, He will draw near to us (see James 4:8).

> Encounters are not limited to certain denominations. God invites everyone to draw near to Him, with the promise that when we do, He will draw near to us.

An example of encounters not being limited to certain people can be found in Acts 9, where Saul of Tarsus encountered Jesus on the Damascus Road. Saul, who was not then a follower of Jesus, was persecuting believers. As a matter of fact, at the time of the encounter Saul was on his way to arrest and execute believers in Jesus. This Damascus Road encounter brought Saul into saving faith in Jesus Christ. Encountering Jesus is necessary for salvation. We encounter Jesus, our Redeemer, which brings us to surrender, repentance, and salvation. When Saul encountered Jesus, his life was completely transformed and he became Paul the apostle.

Another important aspect of Saul's encounter was its effect on the men who were with him. They, too, experienced a measure of supernatural encounter: "The men traveling with him stood speechless, hearing the voice, but seeing no one" (Acts 9:7).

Fourth, encounters are marked by an overwhelming presence of God. Our natural senses give way to our spiritual senses, allowing us to engage in the moment. Don't overlook those encounters that might be more subtle. Anytime heaven invades earth, a measure of encounter has taken place.

Glory Intrusions

Another key characteristic of encounters is the intrusion or appearance of a word or presence from the supernatural realm into the earthly domain. The appearance might be an angel of the Lord bringing a message. Or it might be a direct message, or an intense glory moment like the globe encounter I experienced. In Scripture, face-to-face encounters are common. As I mentioned, God "came down" in the cool of the day (i.e., in the evening) to commune with His son and daughter, Adam and Eve. God appeared to Moses in the burning bush (see Exodus 3). My intent here is not to stereotype or limit these awesome moments, but to provide a point of reference to help us recognize and understand them.

Over the past several years, I have been hearing an increasing number of testimonies about supernatural encounters with the Living God. We now have more books on the subject. The current generation is being marked by glory intrusions. I believe these supernatural moments will and should become common among believers. Like Adam and Eve, we will fellowship with God "in the cool of the day."

Get ready to wear the glory of God in a new way! This is God's manifesto, that we might live in the earth from the realm of encounters.

In divine-human encounters, we are confronted with reality from God's perspective. There are some who incorrectly suppose that we are orphans alone in the universe, absent the presence of a divine Creator who is also our Father. Nothing could be further from the truth. God is mindful of us (see Psalm 8:4). Another way to perceive this is through the lens of what makes up the "father nature." Good fathers spend time with their children. God is a doting Father who enjoys spending time with us. Good fathers instruct their children. When we encounter the Living God, He teaches us about Himself. He reveals Himself. Good fathers protect their children. We are always under the protection of God (see Psalm 34:17–19).

> **Encounters are immensely intimate. Our spiritual senses are heightened, allowing us to perceive in ways beyond our human, earthly capacity.**

Encounters not only lead us to God, but they also unveil His plan and intentions for us. In the midst of an encounter with God, providential and redemptive aspects of His nature and character are made plain. Encounters are immensely intimate. Our spiritual senses are heightened, allowing us to perceive in ways beyond our human, earthly capacity. We are not suspended in time, unaware of our surroundings, in a zombie-like state. We are communing with the Living God in ways that forever change us. In this heavenly realm, time seems nonexistent. In these moments, the only thing that matters is the One whose eyes are as flames of fire (see Revelation 19:12).

Knowing Him

There is a desire in the heart of God for us to know Him. Look at Numbers 12:5–7 (ERV):

> The LORD came down in the tall cloud and stood at the entrance to the Tent. He called out, "Aaron and Miriam!" They went to Him. God said, "Listen to me! You will have prophets. I, the LORD, will let them learn about me through visions. I will speak to them in dreams. But Moses is not like that. He is my faithful servant—I trust him with everyone in my house."

There is also a cry to know Him coming from the hearts of the sons and daughters of the Kingdom. Paul the apostle uttered the same cry—"that I may know him" (Philippians 3:10 KJV).

God wants us to know Him and brings us into encounters to accomplish His desire. His character, personality, and ways are inexhaustible. Therefore, we cannot fully know Him. However, encounters provide us with the opportunity to glimpse Him. We are given a momentary front-row seat in the supernatural realm. An important issue is learning to live supernaturally. I call this living "supernaturally natural," which is the subject of chapter 2. This is the place where engaging heaven becomes as natural as engaging in the earth.

Although we are assigned to life in the earth, engagement at the level of God-encounters is possible because our spirit is eternal and has the capacity to perceive and commune with Him. As we go through the day, we must cultivate our ability to perceive and engage heaven. There is a longing in the heart of our heavenly Father to be known. This is His manifesto—to be known by those He created in His image and likeness.

Living a life of encountering God is more than an attempt of our mere human will to engage the eternal realm of heaven. Rather, this is an intentional pursuit of the One who has purposed us for this time. Without eternal engagement, we cannot fulfill the mandate of heaven. God purposed you, and apart from regular encounters with Him, you will lack the capacity to fully engage and overcome the darkness.

Encounters create conviction. The result of these moments is a strengthening of our conviction, which has a direct impact on increasing our faith. When our faith increases, we become more productive in our Kingdom mandate. Hebrews 11:6 states, "And without faith it is impossible to please God, for he who comes to God must believe that He exists and that He is a rewarder of those who diligently seek Him." God rewards our pursuit of Him by revealing Himself to us. This results in our continued progression in His agenda. In the next chapter, we will discuss more about the supernatural realm and how to begin living regularly in this realm.

PRAYER ACTIVATION

Heavenly Father, I thank You that You have given me access to You through the gateway of supernatural encounters. I believe that You desire to reveal aspects of Yourself to me. Help me perceive Your presence in the smallest ways. Open my ears so I might hear Your whisper. Open my eyes so I might see Your glorious presence. Touch my heart and activate faith in me to believe that not only do You want to encounter me, but that I can encounter You. In Jesus' name, Amen.

TWO

Living Supernaturally Natural

The hearing ear and the seeing eye, the LORD has made both of them.

Proverbs 20:12

We were created with sensory capacity. The hearing ear and the seeing eye give us the capacity to obtain knowledge and understanding. Through our natural senses, we navigate life in the natural world. Our vision, hearing, smell, taste, and touch allow us to sense our environment. Touching the stove immediately after cooking informs us that the stove is hot. The smell of spoiled milk or the softness of a cucumber well beyond the expiration date informs us that they are not safe to consume. Our natural senses help us navigate the world around us, yet they cannot help us navigate the spiritual realm.

"But the natural man does not receive the things of the Spirit of God, for they are foolishness to him; nor can he know them, because they are spiritually discerned" (1 Corinthians 2:14). The natural man or woman is dependent on what can be perceived through the natural mind, rendering him or her incapable of perceiving spiritual things. Prior to salvation, our minds are unregenerated and are unable to perceive spiritual things. Adam Clarke makes the following statements in his commentary on Matthew–Revelation:

> The animal man—the man who is in a mere state of nature, and lives under the influence of his animal passions . . . is not only one who either has had no spiritual teaching or has not profited by it; but one who lives for the present world, having no respect to spiritual or eternal things. . . . He considers it the highest wisdom to live for this world. Therefore, these spiritual things are foolishness to him; for while he is in his animal state, he cannot see their excellency for they are spiritually discerned, and he has no spiritual mind.[1]

We have been given the spiritual enablement to navigate the spiritual realm. God has given us spiritual senses of sight, sound, smell, hearing, taste, and touch that help us perceive the spirit realm. For example, Psalm 34:8 invites us to "taste and see" that the Lord is good. Matthew 13:9 says, "Whoever has ears to hear, let him hear." We are spiritual beings living in an earthly body. We were created to experience heaven during our time on earth as human beings. But this can only be done through our spiritual senses. As with any physical capacity, functioning in the supernatural realm can and should be cultivated. Living supernaturally must become natural. This is the realm of encounters.

A Look at Our Human Design

Let's look more closely at our human design. We are triune beings created spirit, soul, and body. Our design includes the supernatural capacity to sense and know God. Paul wrote, "May the very God of peace sanctify you completely. And I pray to God that your whole spirit, soul, and body be preserved blameless unto the coming of our Lord Jesus Christ" (1 Thessalonians 5:23). Spiritual things cannot be understood through our natural mind; they must be discerned and understood through our spiritual mind.

> **We are triune beings created spirit, soul, and body. Our design includes the supernatural capacity to sense and know God.**

Supernatural encounters with the Living God are not earth events. They are spiritual and can only be understood through our spiritual mind. As I said, the natural part of us does not comprehend the things of the spirit. Yet because God made us with three parts, we can comprehend things in the spiritual realm. Looking at each of our three parts in a little more detail will help us understand this more fully.[2]

The Spirit

Your spirit, which is eternal, is the first part of your being and includes your spiritual mind. You were created to fellowship with God, who is Spirit. The part of your nature that communicates with God is your eternal spirit. Scripture refers to this part of your nature as the "inward man" or the "hidden man of the heart" (see Romans 7:22). As I wrote in a previous book, *Next-Level Believers*,

> The spirit part of us, the "spirit of man," refers to our heart. In 1 Peter 3:3–4, Peter was referring to the human spirit when he talked about the "hidden nature of the heart":

> Do not let your adorning be the outward adorning
> of braiding the hair, wearing gold, or putting on fine
> clothing. But let it be the hidden nature of the heart,
> that which is not corruptible, even the ornament of
> a gentle and quiet spirit, which is very precious in
> the sight of God.

Just as it is today, outward adornment was many people's focus in those days. Peter exhorted the Church not merely to be concerned with outward adorning, but with what was on the inside.[3]

The Word of God tells us that we are to be kept blameless spirit, soul, and body (see 1 Thessalonians 5:23). This spirit part of you is the part that receives eternal life and has the capacity to access God. Whenever you access God, this is an encounter. Here are a few additional Scriptures that help illustrate this principle:

> For God so loved the world that He gave His only begotten
> Son, that whoever believes in Him should not perish, but
> have eternal life (John 3:16).

> I give them eternal life. They shall never perish, nor shall
> anyone snatch them from My hand (John 10:28).

> This is eternal life: that they may know You, the only true
> God, and Jesus Christ, whom You have sent (John 17:3).

> Paul, a servant of God and an apostle of Jesus Christ, ac-
> cording to the faith of God's elect and the knowledge of
> the truth which leads to godliness, in hope of eternal life
> which God, who cannot lie, promised before the world began
> (Titus 1:1–2).

As I said, people are spiritual beings who live in a natural body. We were created in the image and likeness of God as cognizant, intellectual beings who have the capacity to communicate with Him. In the same way that God came down "in the cool of the day" to commune with Adam and Eve, He desires to commune with us. Kenneth Hagin commented about this,

> "God is a Spirit: and they that worship him must worship him in spirit and in truth" (John 4:24). We cannot know God or touch Him physically. He is not a man. He is Spirit. We cannot communicate with God mentally, for He is a Spirit. But we can reach Him with our spirit, and it is through our spirit that we come to know God.[4]

When we become born again, we gain the capacity to access and understand spiritual things. As Hagin says, we come to know God through our spirit.

Everything we experience is filtered through natural thought processes, however. We will look more at this in the following section on the soul, but the importance of our minds can be seen in the fact that the Bible mentions the mind more than two hundred times. In the Amplified version of the Bible, there are actually 233 references to the mind. Here are a few of those passages:

> For those who are living according to the flesh set their minds on the things of the flesh [which gratify the body], but those who are living according to the Spirit, [set their minds on] the things of the Spirit [His will and purpose]. Now the mind of the flesh is death [both now and forever—because it pursues sin]; but the mind of the Spirit is life and peace [the spiritual well-being that comes from walking with God—both now and forever] (Romans 8:5–6 AMP).

For who has known the mind and purposes of the LORD, so as to instruct Him? But we have the mind of Christ [to be guided by His thoughts and purposes] (1 Corinthians 2:16 AMP).

The god of this world [Satan] has blinded the minds of the unbelieving to prevent them from seeing the illuminating light of the gospel of the glory of Christ, who is the image of God (2 Corinthians 4:4 AMP).

And be continually renewed in the spirit of your mind [having a fresh, untarnished mental and spiritual attitude] (Ephesians 4:23 AMP).

Yet it is through our human spirit that we encounter God. As I explained in *Next-Level Believers*,

Your inner man is the real person inside. Your outward man—the person of flesh and bones, your body—is not the real person. Your inward man—the eternal part of you—is the real person who will never die. "Even though our outward man is perishing, yet our inward man is being renewed day by day" (2 Corinthians 4:16).[5]

When we understand these truths, we can live in a state of being alert and tuned in to the spiritual realm, where we encounter God. If not, we live in a state in which our natural senses of taste, touch, sight, hearing, and smell are primarily tuned in to our human existence.

The Soul

I explained this about the soul in *Next-Level Believers*:

The soul is the seat of human intellect. It is the place where our mind, will and emotions reside. Your soul is the realm of your sensibilities and will, and it is the part of you that reasons and thinks. It deals with your mental realm. Your soul must continually be submitted to the Spirit of God.[6]

An unsubmitted soul results in carnal living (see Romans 7:14; 8:1–6). *Vine's Expository Dictionary of Biblical Words* defines *carnal* as, "Having the nature of flesh, i.e., sensual, controlled by animal appetites, governed by our human nature, instead of by the Holy Spirit."[7] Living carnally does not produce the life of Christ. According to *Clarke's Commentary*, "A carnal mind relishes earthly and sinful things, and lives in opposition to the pure and holy law of God: therefore, it is enmity against God: it is irreconcilable."[8] The apostle Paul admonished us as believers to allow the Holy Spirit to transform us inwardly through a total reformation of our thinking:

> Stop imitating the ideals and opinions of the culture around you, but be inwardly transformed by the Holy Spirit through a total reformation of how you think. This will empower you to discern God's will as you live a beautiful life, satisfying and perfect in his eyes.
>
> Romans 12:2 TPT

I also wrote this about the transformation of our mind:

> Your mind is a key battleground of the enemy. If he captures your thoughts, it hinders your walk with Christ. Proverbs 23:7 states, "for as he [any person] thinks in his heart, so is he." The soul is the center of our mind, will, intellect, emotions, etc. Each day, you and I must commit to the transformation of our soul so that we are not conformed to the

pattern of the culture. Our current culture has become hedonistic and self-serving. Even among those of us who profess faith in Christ, the transformation of our mind, leading to reformation of our lives, is too often shallow or nonexistent. Our lives must be reflective of the power of Christ working within us. The apostle Paul's message exhorted early believers that their experience with Christ must extend to the transformation of their entire lives. This fact has not changed. Your profession of faith in Christ must result in total transformation of your life.[9]

Your soul must be submitted to the Lord daily throughout your life. When you encounter the supernatural realm of heaven, transformation is possible. These moments of interaction with the heavenly realm have great transformational impact.

It is important to note that while we consider encounters to be deeply spiritual experiences that occur among believers, the reality is that supernatural encounters can also occur in the life of unbelievers. God, who is not willing that any should perish, but who desires that all would come to repentance (see 2 Peter 3:9), encountered Saul of Tarsus while he was en route to Damascus to execute followers of Jesus Christ. As we saw in Acts 9, this supernatural encounter with the Living Jesus changed Saul's life. Prior to his encounter with Jesus, Saul was a Pharisee who was focused on persecuting the Church (see Philippians 3:3–6). This supernatural encounter became the catalyst for his transformation into becoming a follower of Jesus Christ! In Saul's case, the encounter led him to a profession of faith in Christ and to becoming one of the foremost apostles in the Bible. Supernatural encounters are transformational.

The Body

Now take a look at my explanation of the body from *Next-Level Believers*:

> The third dimension of humanity is the natural man, or our human bodies. Unlike the spirit and soul, which are eternal, the natural body is not. The natural body is the "earth house" where our spirit and soul reside during our time on earth. The body, the natural aspect, has a span of time to exist in the earth, after which a person lives eternally in the spirit realm. Your body must be submitted daily to the Holy Spirit:
>
> > I urge you therefore, brothers, by the mercies of God, that you present your bodies as a living sacrifice, holy, and acceptable to God, which is your reasonable service of worship (Romans 12:1).
>
> The apostle Paul exhorted believers to submit their bodies to the Lord as their reasonable act of worship. This is something all believers are expected to do. Paul did not say to the Church, "Pray and ask the Lord to make your body a living sacrifice." Rather, they were instructed to surrender themselves to God.[10]

The principle of sacrifice is clearly woven throughout Scripture. After Adam and Eve transgressed in the Garden of Eden, "The LORD God made tunics of [animal] skins for Adam and his wife and clothed them" (Genesis 3:21 AMP; see also Genesis 31:54; Exodus 5:3; 2 Chronicles 5; 7; Psalm 4:5; 50:5; 51; Hebrews 13:15–16). Submission to Christ requires the sacrifice of our life for His, our agenda for His. This is the principle of sacrifice.

Before salvation, our habits and ways of living didn't align with the Kingdom of God. Our ungodly habits were reflective of the kingdom of darkness, as Galatians 5:18–21 (TPT) shows:

> But when you yield to the life of the Spirit, you will no longer be living under the law, but soaring above it!
> The behavior of the self-life is obvious: Sexual immorality, lustful thoughts, pornography, chasing after things instead of God, manipulating others, hatred of those who get in your way, senseless arguments, resentment when others are favored, temper tantrums, angry quarrels, only thinking of yourself, being in love with your own opinions, being envious of the blessings of others, murder, uncontrolled addictions, wild parties, and all other similar behavior.

Again, we are triune beings—spirit, soul, and body. It is through our spiritual mind that we experience supernatural encounters. The problem, however, is our dependence on our natural mind to process all information. Spiritual things cannot be fully understood by our natural mind. You must renew your mind daily through the Word of God. This is how transformation happens. Your thoughts create your perception. Through your mind you process life events and experiences, which then influence your perception. Your mind is more than the brain in your body functioning as an amazing computer processor, storing events that occur in your life. Your mind is a gateway. Paul admonished us as believers to cultivate the mind of Christ: "Let this mind be in you all, which was also in Christ Jesus" (Philippians 2:5).

Necessary, but Not Automatic

Living supernaturally natural is necessary, but not automatic. The daily submission of our lives is the prerequisite to living in the supernatural realm. Adam lived in this realm prior to the Fall in the Garden. He was connected to the supernatural realm, and his clothing was a glory suit. There was no need for another type of clothing, because the glory of God covered him. He communed (fellowshiped) with God in the evening. Adam's ability to name every living thing was connected to his living supernaturally natural. He could name the lion because he knew that heaven called the lion "lion." Renewing your mind through prayer, worship, and the study of God's Word will clear the mental debris that is collected and stored in our minds.

Another way to understand living supernaturally natural can be seen in Adam's life in the Garden. The Garden represents our portion. We each have been given a portion to tend. Just as with a natural garden where weeding and watering are necessary functions for growth and multiplication, when we live supernaturally natural, our capacity to represent God in the earth increases. This requires intentionality. Too many believers think they will "automatically grow" or "automatically function supernaturally." Yet in the same manner that a garden requires care, your spiritual development requires intentional care. Nothing should be left to chance.

> In the same manner that a garden requires care, your spiritual development requires intentional care. Nothing should be left to chance.

I encourage you to start watching and listening for heaven's interruptions in your life. One of the names of God is *Jehovah Shammah*, meaning "the Lord is there." God is waiting for you to step fully into the realm of the supernatural with Him. Stop thinking that living supernaturally natural is for others, but not for you.

Nothing could be further from the truth. Incredible journeys with God await you. Are you ready?

PRAYER ACTIVATION

Lord, I thank You that I am made in Your image and in Your likeness. You have given me a hearing ear and a seeing eye. I have the capacity to perceive Your presence and to hear Your voice. I commit to intentionally drawing closer to You so that I can commune with You. Help me recognize heaven's interruptions in my life. I am ready to step into the realm of the supernatural. Help me not to miss divine moments with You, in Jesus' name.

THREE

The Supernatural Advantage

The LORD appeared to Abram and said, "To your descendants I will give this land." So he built an altar to the LORD,
who had appeared to him.

Genesis 12:7

Looking at the life of Abraham, we see an ordinary individual
who encountered God in an extraordinary way. Abraham's
encounters with God paved the way for his transformation
from Abram (meaning "exalted father") to Abraham (meaning "father of a multitude"). Let's not miss this point: In the
Old Testament, a person's name often signified his or her
prophetic identity. As one example, according to *Strong's
Hebrew Lexicon*, the name *Adam* means "a human being
(an individual or the species, mankind, etc.)."[1] God created
the first human as *Adam*, or *man*.

Likewise, Abram's name was a prophetic identifier. He
was childless, yet prophetically his name meant "exalted
father." His name was a clue to his destiny before his first
son, Ishmael, was born. Encounters with God gave him a

supernatural advantage over his enemies, as well as an advantage in life. Abram became Abraham, and he went from being an exalted father of one son, Ishmael, who was born through his wife Sarah's servant Hagar, to becoming the father of Isaac, who was later born through Sarah herself. Not only that, but history also records six more sons he fathered who were born through another wife, Keturah, after Sarah's death (see Genesis 25:2). This is a picture of the supernatural advantage operating in Abraham's life.

As believers, you and I have this same advantage as Abraham, yet we don't always realize our supernatural blessings. The importance of understanding the supernatural realm has been grossly understated. This lack of understanding impedes our capacity to understand how to engage on a higher spiritual level. In chapter 2, we discussed the three parts we are created with as human beings—spirit, soul, and body. As we saw, our eternal spirit part is designed to commune with God on a supernatural level. This fact alone informs us of the importance of cultivating our human spirit to sense and engage with the presence of God.

A Supernatural Encounter

One time I was traveling from Charleston, South Carolina, to Dallas, Texas, to attend a conference hosted by Apostle Chuck Pierce. I had already been traveling for a few days and was very tired. Almost immediately after boarding the plane, I fell asleep. Very soon, I shifted from sleep to a supernatural encounter. I have noted that often when I experience vision or dream encounters, it appears as though I am watching the events on a movie screen. While I was asleep, I saw the screen appear. The scene was the plane I was traveling on. I could see my assistant, who was sitting across the aisle from me.

In the vision, she was talking with the passenger sitting next to her. In reality, she was watching a movie on her device.

Next in the encounter, I noticed the person sitting next to me, who was now wearing what looked like a black ninja outfit. Only his eyes could be seen. I was sitting in the aisle seat. He then shifted from sitting to my immediate right to sitting between me and the passenger in front of me (this plane had rear-facing seats). Rather than facing the front of the plane, he was now facing backward. As I watched events unfold, I noticed that he was chanting over and over. I attempted to alert my assistant, who was distracted by the conversation she was engaged in. I reached across the aisle to touch her and say, "He's chanting! He's chanting!"

My assistant looked at him momentarily, and quickly returned to her conversation. Again, I reached across the aisle and tapped her hand. I said to her again, "He's chanting! He's chanting!"

At this point, the man in black stopped chanting and picked up his phone, attempting to contact one of his demonic superiors. He was met with interference by whoever or whatever was at the other end of the call. I heard him say, "Put me through to them! I do have the authority! Not only do I have the authority, but I'm also good at what I do, and I like it. I have the authority—now put me through!"

The scene then went dark, and I awakened. Immediately, I noticed that the heavy fatigue I had been experiencing was gone. I felt fully refreshed. I pondered the supernatural events that had just occurred. Remember, encounters must be interpreted through the lens of Scripture. Over the next few days, I continued to consider the meaning of the vision. I was scheduled to return home from the Texas conference on Sunday. Saturday evening, the Lord spoke to me and said, *Do not return home without sharing the vision.*

Share it? I thought. I wasn't even sure what it meant. I arrived at the final service I would attend on Sunday morning and continued to ponder how and when to share the vision. The worship was incredible. Apostle Chuck Pierce, who was hosting the meeting, declared, "New Orleans will experience revival!"

Immediately, I heard the Holy Spirit instruct me that the moment to share the vision had arrived. I walked onto the stage and began to share how earlier in the week, the Spirit of God had spoken the word *conclave* to me. I went on to share the meaning of the word, which is a private meeting or secret assembly. I then shared the vision. It was then that the interpretation came to me, which I also shared: "There has been a demonic gathering of witches and warlocks who have released a new demonic frequency into the earth. Demonic curses, declarations, hexes, etc., have stirred the atmosphere of the earth. This diabolical frequency of hell has been released upon the earth to wage war against the Body of Christ more extensively in the upcoming year. The Body of Christ must continually access the frequency of heaven, which will enable us to override the frequency of hell and walk in new levels of victory and breakthrough. Our senses must be tuned to heaven's frequency!"

The vision was an alert to the Body of Christ concerning the escalation of demonic activity, and was giving instruction concerning what we must do in the days ahead to be victorious over any and every attack.

Secrets Revealed

Daniel understood the supernatural advantage. In Daniel 2, we read that King Nebuchadnezzar had dreamed a dream that troubled him. When the king awakened from sleep, he was unable to recall the dream, yet he remained troubled. After summoning the magicians, astrologers, and sorcerers who served in the palace, he instructed them not only to give him the interpretation of the dream, but also to tell him the dream itself—which they could not do. King Nebuchadnezzar explained to them that their failure would result in their deaths and the destruction of their homes. Angry over the wise men's failure to tell him the dream and interpret it, the king ordered the execution of all the wise men in Babylon.

Although Daniel was not a magician, astrologer, or sorcerer, he was assigned to work in the palace and therefore faced the same sentence of death. He needed a supernatural advantage, so he and his friends started praying:

> Then Daniel went to his house and made the thing known to Hananiah, Mishael, and Azariah, his companions, so that they might ask for compassion from the God of heaven concerning this secret, so that Daniel and his companions might not perish with the rest of the wise men of Babylon.
>
> Daniel 2:17–18

Prayer activates the supernatural advantage. Look what the next verse tells us: "Then the secret was revealed to Daniel in a night vision. Then Daniel blessed the God of heaven" (verse 19). Through his supernatural advantage, Daniel was able not only to interpret the king's dream, but also first to tell the king the dream itself. This is how the supernatural advantage works on our behalf. We have access to information we would not otherwise know. "The secret things belong to the LORD our God, but those things which are revealed belong to us and to our children forever, so that we may keep all the words of this law" (Deuteronomy 29:29).

The need to live in the supernatural realm, where we experience regular spiritual encounters, cannot be overstated. Supernatural encounters transform us. It is advantageous for every believer to access this realm on a consistent basis. "But we all, seeing the glory of the Lord with unveiled faces, as in a mirror, are being transformed into the same image from glory to glory by the Spirit of the Lord" (2 Corinthians 3:18). The key is not to be pursuing spiritual encounters, but to be pursuing God Himself. Daniel sought for God, who is the revealer of secrets. Throughout Scripture, we see how the God of heaven appeared to men and women to make known His plans. He was, in fact, giving them a supernatural advantage.

The need to live in the supernatural realm, where we experience regular spiritual encounters, cannot be overstated. Supernatural encounters transform us.

The Snare of Humanism

One of the dangers of the modern-day Church is the spirit of independence, which is linked with the spirit of humanism. These spirits are diabolical. Their overall goal is to influence individuals toward self-reliance and independence from God. People under the influence of humanism overlook the need for dependence on God, choosing to trust their own minds and opinions. They are often void of faith in the Living God.

These spirits of humanism and independence attempt to create distance between you and God, creating the deceptive illusion that He is not present with you, and that since He is inaccessible, you are free to make decisions and choices based on your own philosophies. It is true that we are free to choose and decide things; however, every decision has a consequence. Decisions based on God's Word and His will result in the manifestation of His promises in our lives. In contrast, decisions based on human intellect alone do not result in the manifestation of His promises. Remember, one of the names of God I talked about is *Jehovah Shammah*, meaning "the Lord is there." God is not with us in a passive way. His Word, *Logos*, the Bible, is alive.

God is also with us through the indwelling Holy Spirit. This is another type of encounter in which believers progressively come to know the Person and work of the Holy Spirit. We must learn His voice and His operations. "But the Counselor, the Holy Spirit, whom the Father will send in My name, will teach you everything and remind you of all that I told you" (John 14:26). We must walk in the power of the Holy Spirit. The Holy Spirit is our Teacher. He reveals the patterns and principles of the supernatural realm as we yield ourselves to Him. We should understand and pursue spiritual things, beginning with our knowledge of Him.

> **The Holy Spirit is our Teacher. He reveals the patterns and principles of the supernatural realm as we yield ourselves to Him.**

Supernatural Words

You and I were created for relationship with God and with each other. I quoted 1 Corinthians 2:14 in the previous chapter, but now let's look at it in a different translation, the Amplified Bible:

> But the natural [unbelieving] man does not accept the things [the teachings and revelations] of the Spirit of God, for they

are foolishness [absurd and illogical] to him; and he is incapable of understanding them, because they are spiritually discerned and appreciated, [and he is unqualified to judge spiritual matters].

Spiritual things must be understood through the Spirit of God. Therefore, God gives us spiritual language to understand spiritual things:

> We also speak of these things, not in words taught or supplied by human wisdom, but in those taught by the Spirit, combining, and interpreting spiritual thoughts with spiritual words [for those being guided by the Holy Spirit].
>
> 1 Corinthians 2:13 AMP

Those who are spiritual men and women can comprehend the things of the Spirit. A way to further understand this principle is through an understanding of the prophetic realm. This is a supernatural realm whereby we encounter heaven through audible expressions, visions, dreams, and the like that God gives.

The prophetic realm is connected to the unseen realm of heaven. This is the realm beyond our natural senses of sight, touch, taste, smell, and hearing. It is a realm that is spiritually discerned. This is the realm where Adam and Eve walked with God. Although they lived in the natural, earthly Garden, their senses were tuned to the spiritual realm: "And they heard the voice of the LORD God walking in the garden in the cool of the day" (Genesis 3:8 KJV). Adam and Eve heard the voice of God. These were moments of supernatural encounter with Him. They fellowshiped with God "in the cool of the day." Their spiritual ears and senses were tuned to the spiritual realm, and it gave them the capacity to hear God walking in the Garden. They could perceive His presence.

Then their transgression in the Garden resulted in Adam and Eve no longer being "God conscious." Now they were "self-conscious." The glory of the Lord that previously covered them as a garment was no longer upon them. Now they could see what they had not seen before—their nakedness. For the first time, they had become aware of themselves. They experienced something that they had never experienced before—self-focus. This is how they were able to recognize their nakedness. Since they had been clothed in God's glory, they had previously been unaware of being naked. Now that they knew they were naked, they began to feel vulnerable, as if they were on their own. Gaining self-focus instilled fear and destroyed trust. Adam and Eve were no longer at peace.

But God did not abandon them. God came walking "in the cool of the day," as He had done before. He expressed His loving heart toward Adam and Eve as He provided clothing for them to cover their nakedness. As God spoke to them about future events, they were touching the prophetic realm, albeit from a different position. The apostle Paul experienced this realm when he described being swept away and taken into the third heaven (see 2 Corinthians 12:2). When we touch prophetic realms, we touch the supernatural. The prophetic realm allows us to access revelatory insights and information that we might not otherwise know. The source of this information is God.

> The prophetic realm allows us to access revelatory insights and information that we might not otherwise know. The source of this information is God.

We must also be aware, however, that another source of information comes from the demonic realm, where Satan operates. This is where psychics and occult powers keep their domain. Because this source of information is from the kingdom of darkness, it is a source forbidden to believers.

Mysteries Revealed

Touching prophetic realms is a supernatural encounter that gives us access to the mysteries of heaven. Look again at Deuteronomy 29:29: "The secret things belong to the LORD our God, but those things which are revealed belong to us and to our children forever, so that we may keep all the words of this law." This was the realm the apostle Paul experienced when he heard mysteries of heaven that were not lawful for him to repeat (see 2 Corinthians 12:4). As believers, you and I also have access to these realms. Throughout our life and walk as believers, we will face challenges to our destiny and our Kingdom assignment. Our continuity in our walk to our destiny requires supernatural encounters. Through regular encounters with Jesus, our Redeemer, our stability increases.

Before you dismiss the need for regular supernatural encounters, consider the dynamic of prayer. Through prayer, we encounter the voice and presence of the Lord Jesus, or at least we should. Encounters will help you overcome discouragement and will give you the stability you need. We should value and depend on encounters more than we depend on dry, religious rhetoric, which lacks power.

Too many believers have no idea how to touch prophetic realms, or how to engage heaven to gain insights into the heart and intents of God and His purposes for them. God has created humanity to interact with Himself. If you are unlearned in the area of prophecy, I encourage you to attend schools of the Spirit, facilitated by mature men and women of God. Moments of prophetic encounter await you. Here are two principles to help you to activate your faith for prophetic encounters:

- *Be prayerful.* Just as God communed with Adam and Eve during the cool of the day, He delights in communing with you during your prayer time. Don't miss your moments of encounter, because God still speaks.
- *Wait, and expect encounters.* Be intentional about spending time waiting for God to speak to you. Not only will God speak to you during your prayer time, but you can also experience His voice all throughout the day and night. This is how we receive words of warning or instruction. God's voice is heard in our "spirit man." Once you become accustomed to hearing the voice of the Lord, you will develop the practice of waiting and listening for His voice. Whenever we experience the voice of God, we have encountered Him.

As you engage in prayer, waiting and expecting to encounter God's presence, here are some ways that you may experience supernatural encounters:

- *Dreams.* You can encounter God through dreams. Not all dreams are prophetic, but some of them are. Dream encounters are often quite vivid. These supernatural moments of encounter reveal God's heart concerning you, your city, or your nation. Activate your faith to believe that your dreams can include a God-encounter.

- *Visions.* Visions are slightly different from dreams. While dreams occur while you are sleeping, visions can occur while you are awake or asleep. I make a distinction between dreams and visions. Most often when I experience a vision, it is very much like watching a movie. For me, these moments are direct and to the point, and they don't include many of the nonessential scenes that I experience in a dream. Visions are direct encounters with God.

- *Worship.* Worship opens up the supernatural realm. Having worship music on and spending time in worship is important to "preparing the atmosphere" so we can hear God. How often have you engaged in prayer, only to notice that your mind has been everywhere except in the place of prayer? Worship helps us bring our minds to a place of stillness in the prayer room so that we are receptive to the voice of the Lord. Like Adam and Eve, in the stillness we can "walk with God in the cool of the day." God longs for us to join Him there. There are also supernatural worship encounters where you experience the worship of heaven. In such encounters, you may hear the angels singing. Another encounter may happen when a new prophetic song you have never heard before arises in your spirit. This kind of worship encounter is activated through your worship.

Remember that God wants you to touch prophetic realms and access information from His heart. Such moments of supernatural encounter can become regular occurrences in your life. The key is expectant faith.

PRAYER ACTIVATION

Heavenly Father, I thank You for giving me the supernatural advantage. Teach me how to use the advantage You have given me. Help me discern when You are speaking to me. Alert me when I am in an encounter dream. Help me pursue You above all else so that I might have more visions and dreams that help me understand Your intentions for me, my family, and my nation. In Jesus' name, Amen.

FOUR

Legal versus Illegal Encounters

> On one occasion, as we went to the place of prayer, a servant girl possessed with a spirit of divination met us, who brought her masters much profit by fortune-telling.
>
> Acts 16:16

Satan rules in the darkness within an infrastructure of principalities, powers, rulers of the darkness, and spiritual forces of evil in the heavenly places. Unlike God, Satan is not omnipresent. He cannot be everywhere at the same time. He utilizes a diabolical infrastructure of principalities, powers, rulers, and spiritual forces to promote his agenda.

Beyond his infrastructure, Satan influences human beings to give their allegiance to him. He is the antithesis of the Most High God. God offers us the abundant life. Satan, who is a thief, comes only to steal, kill, and destroy. As Jesus tells us in John 10:10, "The thief does not come, except to steal and kill and destroy. I came that they may have life, and that they may have it more abundantly."

Jesus is "the way, the truth, and the life" (John 14:6). Satan is "the father of lies" (John 8:44).

Two Spiritual Kingdoms

There are two spiritual kingdoms operating in the earth—the Kingdom of God, and the kingdom of Satan. All human beings are citizens of one of these two kingdoms. Kingdoms do not operate without a structure. For example, consider nations like Great Britain, whose governmental structure includes a king and queen. In his book *Rediscovering the Kingdom*, pastor and international speaker Dr. Myles Munroe states,

> It is most important to note that God our Creator chose the concept of a kingdom to communicate His purpose, will and plan for mankind and earth to us. The message of the Bible is primarily and obviously about a Kingdom. If you do not understand kingdoms, it is impossible for you to understand the Bible and its message.[1]

To show the importance of understanding the concept of a kingdom, consider that the Modern English Version of the Bible references *kingdom* 569 times. The fact that *kingdom* is mentioned this often in the Bible implies that believers should spend time in study and prayer to understand this concept. The following list describing kingdoms has been adapted from Dr. Monroe's book.[2]

- A King and Lord—a sovereign; the ruler possessing ultimate authority over the kingdom. Whoever possesses the gates of the Kingship possesses the Kingdom (presidency, judiciary, and legislature; see Isaiah 33:22).

- A Territory—refers to the territory over which the king rules.
- A Constitution—the covenant of a king with his citizenry; it expresses the mind and will of the king for his citizens and kingdom. Another way to say this is to understand the concept of a manifesto.
- A Citizenry—a community of subjects; those who are subjects of the king.
- Law—acceptable principles by which all citizens are governed.
- Privileges—rights and benefits that can be enjoyed by all citizens.
- A Code of Ethics—details an acceptable lifestyle and conduct for citizens within the kingdom.
- An Army—security, and protection forces for the territory and its citizens.
- A Commonwealth—economic financial security for citizens of the kingdom.
- A Social Culture—protocol and procedures that separate the king and his citizens from other kings and territories.

In *Next-Level Believers*, I gave this explanation of Satan's kingdom and how the spiritual forces of evil work through the fallen systems and kingdoms of the world today:

> Satan is the ruler of the kingdom of darkness, where, according to Ephesians 6:12, a hierarchal structure of principalities, powers and rulers of darkness exists. The spiritual beings in the kingdom of darkness consist of demons and all the people who live in sin and rebellion to God's Word. Through the fallen systems and kingdoms of the natural world, the

kingdom of darkness seeks to enslave humanity through the lust of flesh, the lust of the eyes and the pride of life. These spiritual forces of evil are at work in the world today.[3]

I also quoted 1 John 2:15–17 (TPT), which I want to quote again for you here. This Scripture illustrates that we need to understand which Kingdom we are citizens of, and which kingdom we are not.

> Don't set the affections of your heart on this world or in loving the things of the world. The love of the Father and the love of the world are incompatible. For all that the world can offer us—the gratification of our flesh, the allurement of the things of the world, and the obsession with status and importance—none of these things come from the Father but from the world. This world and its desires are in the process of passing away, but those who love to do the will of God live forever.

Illegal Access

Encounters with God are not the only encounters occurring in the spirit realm. Encounters are supernatural and can be initiated either by God or Satan. I caution you to discern and examine encounters through the Word of God. It is only through understanding the nature and character of God, which is revealed in Scripture, that you can discern the origin of any encounter. Encounters are moments of revelation. They are deeply spiritual moments. We don't leave encounters in the same way we entered.

God-initiated encounters reveal truth to us pertaining to His will. These are also moments of impartation, healing, deliverance, and breakthrough. But Satan is a counterfeit being who also looks for opportunities to encounter human beings. His purpose is to deceive and seduce you. Another tactic of demonically initiated encounters is to bring accusation against God: "Now the serpent was more subtle than any beast of the field which the LORD God had made. And he said to the woman, 'Has God said . . . ?'" (Genesis 3:1). These three words, *Has God said*, are designed to deceive you into questioning God's intentions.

Encounters initiated by the kingdom of darkness can bring much harm. If you don't have a biblical understanding of the nature and character of God, or of the operations of His Kingdom, you can misinterpret a supernatural experience. Encounters initiated by the kingdom of darkness attempt to exalt the agenda of Satan over the agenda of the Most High God. Remember, Satan is seeking rulership and uses deception and lies to accomplish his agenda.

> **Encounters are moments of revelation. They are deeply spiritual moments. We don't leave encounters in the same way we entered.**

Diabolical Counterfeiter

The Bible describes the original position of Satan in Ezekiel 28:12–17. When Satan was originally created, he was an angel of God who was given a position on God's holy mountain and apparently led in worship (see verses 13–14). He was one of the cherubim class of angels, holy, wise, beautiful, and perfect. He was the leader among the cherubs and is called a "guardian" or "covering" cherub.

Satan's name was originally Lucifer, which means "light bearer" (see Isaiah 14:12). A gem has no light of its own. It is not beautiful in a dark room. Its beauty is in its ability to reflect light from without. Satan was meant to reflect God's light. Instead of doing that, however, he still wants to be the supreme ruler in place of the One he was meant to be a reflection of. He is waging an intense battle for the heart, mind, soul, and spirit of men and women everywhere. His strategies are directed at God, His plan, and His people.

Wicked spirits have infiltrated the systems of the world, including the religious system. These systems operate in similar ways to the Kingdom of God. Satan has leaders who operate under the guise of apostles, prophets, pastors, teachers, and evangelists. These wicked rulers have crept into the congregation of the righteous, working to expand the manifesto of the kingdom of darkness. In some cases, Satan actually has congregations known as the "Church of Satan" or "Spiritualists." He has set up a form of worship in spiritual high places.

When you are unlearned in the Word of God and you lack discernment, you are at risk of being deceived into believing that the operations of Satan are the operations of God. This is why encounters must be interpreted through accurate biblical understanding. It is only through the lens of Scripture that we can determine the accuracy of any supernatural encounter.

God's Manifesto

Earlier in this book, I briefly discussed God's manifesto. One definition of a *manifesto* is "a published declaration of intentions, motives, or views of the issuer."[4] A manifesto is a public statement of your intention. Famous civil rights leader Dr. Martin Luther King Jr. had a manifesto of racial equality and social justice that he communicated in his legacy speech, "I Have a Dream."

According to thought leader and business/content expert Geoff McDonald,

> A manifesto is a public statement of your intention. It's a description of how you see the world or want the world to be. But not all manifestos are created equal. Some are more inspiring, more influential, and more well-known than others.[5]

McDonald says that the Bible is considered the most famous manifesto of all time, and that the classic format of a manifesto would be the Ten Commandments, which lay out ten rules on how to live as a Christian.

God's manifesto is clearly superior to all others and includes instructions for life on earth and for fellowship with Him. God describes His patterns and processes in His manifesto, the Bible. He encourages us to draw near to Him, and then He will draw near to us (see James 4:8). His stated manifesto includes relationship and fellowship with us. His intent is for us to live as His sons and daughters, reflecting His character and nature wherever we are.

As a loving Father, God creates moments where we can experience Him intimately. His manifesto of relationship and fellowship is realized during our encounter moments with Him. Encounters with God must be regarded as possible for everyone, a privilege that must be valued, and a priority that should be pursued. Here are three powerful truths that should not be overlooked:

1. We are created in the image and likeness of God.
2. We have the capacity to commune with God.
3. We have been created a little lower than God Himself.

These amazing truths are at the core of why Satan hates us. We have the high privilege of communicating with God through supernatural encounters. These incredible moments are Spirit to spirit—God's Spirit communing with our spirit (see John 4:24). Nothing else in creation has this incredible honor. The psalmist, David, sang this truth in Psalm 8:4–6:

> What is man that You are mindful of him, and the son of man that You attend to him?
> For You have made him a little lower than the angels, and crowned him with glory and honor. You have given him dominion over the works of Your hands; You have put all things under his feet.

Although the biblical translations indicate humankind as being a little lower than the angels, *Strong's Hebrew Lexicon* translates the word *angels* here as *Elohim*, a word that is referenced in the Bible as *God* more than 2,300 times.[6] The meaning here is that human beings were made a little lower than God Himself. We were designed to fulfill God's manifesto of fellowship and communion with Him.

Satan's Manifesto

Satan, or Lucifer, is a counterfeit and copycat who has his own inferior manifesto, which offers death and destruction. We can find the manifesto of Satan described in Isaiah 14:12–17:

> How are you fallen from heaven, O Lucifer, son of the morning! How you are cut down to the ground, you who weaken the nations! For you have said in your heart "I will ascend into heaven, I will exalt my throne above the stars of God; I

will sit also on the mount of the congregation, in the recesses of the north; I will ascend above the heights of the clouds, I will be like the Most High." Yet you shall be brought down to Hell, to the sides of the pit.

Those who see you shall stare at you and ponder over you: "Is this the man who made the earth to tremble and shook kingdoms, who made the world as a wilderness and destroyed its cities, who did not open the house of his prisoners?"

Satan remains determined to become like the Most High. His habitation is in the second heaven. Genesis 1 provides a description for us of how God has structured the heavens. The first heaven is referred to as the atmosphere and includes the air we breathe, and the area immediately surrounding the earth. The second heaven is the solar system; it is in this realm that the powers of darkness dwell. The third heaven is the place where God's throne is established.[7] In my book *Next-Level Spiritual Warfare: Advanced Strategies for Defeating the Enemy* (Chosen, 2019), I describe the habitation of Satan in the second heaven in more detail. Here, however, I want to describe some of the activities Satan engages in from the place where he dwells. Let's look at some of his strategies such as using the occult and psychics, New Age concepts, veiled agendas, and the snare of compromise.

The Occult and Psychics

"For our fight is not against flesh and blood, but against principalities, against powers, against the rulers of the darkness of this world, and against spiritual forces of evil in the heavenly places" (Ephesians 6:12). Through spiritual wickedness in high places, Satan aims to win the total allegiance of humankind. He uses false cults, his own Church of Satan, and infiltration into the Body of Christ to accomplish this purpose. The word *occult* means to hide or conceal a thing.[8] Cults are part of the occult. Within this paradigm, they hide and conceal evil behind the cloak of religion.

The organization of cults is not a recent occurrence. Satan has used false worship systems from the beginning. The Old Testament shows us the continued pattern of false worship systems that ensnared the children of Israel. Worship and allegiance are linked. Whatever we worship, we submit to (see John 14:15, 21). There is a longing for worship within every human being. This is evidenced by the fact of how many religious organizations exist today.

Satan seeks to counterfeit the Kingdom of God. Earlier, we discussed Satan's leadership structure. God uses prophets and prophetic people to reveal His intentions. Satan uses psychics, mediums, witches, and warlocks. Giving psychic readings is an industry ruled by the spirit of mammon, and it has grown exponentially over recent years. According to *Statista* online,

> The market size of the psychic services industry in the United States increased considerably between 2011 and 2022. Starting from a value of 1.9 billion US dollars in 2011, the market size of the industry reached over 2 billion US dollars for the first time in 2019 and became even more valuable in 2022.[9]

You might wonder why the popularity of this demonically inspired industry continues. The human spirit was created for fellowship with God. In other words, we were created for worship. When we don't worship the true and Living God, we will by default embrace a false worship system. We are curious about the future, and we want to know what will happen. We seek answers to the questions, *What is my purpose in life? Why was I created? What does the future hold for me?* God uses prophets to declare His intentions. Satan, however, uses psychics.

You may be wondering what the difference is between prophets and psychics. Prophets are given to us as gifts from God, and their source of information and revelation comes from Him. Psychics are demonically inspired through information from the kingdom of darkness. You must consider the source of any information you receive during a spiritual encounter. Be careful not to create a doctrine or teaching based solely on an encounter. The Word of God must be the foundation for proving or disproving any experience.

A Warning about "Good Vibes"

The apostle Paul encouraged his spiritual son, Timothy, to study the Scriptures. Timothy was a young, emerging apostle. Likewise, I want to encourage young leaders to become students of the Word of God. Having "good vibes" about something is not enough. I have noted the broad acceptance of this phrase and thought I'd use it here. I have also noted the increased use of the phrase "good energy." These terms are associated with the New Age movement. Our foundation of faith must be built on the Word of God, not on the popular mantras of modern culture.

One dictionary defines *good vibes* this way:

> One early instance of *good vibrations* used in a metaphysical sense for "positive energy" occurs in Frank Earl Ormsby's astrology 1893 text *The Law and the Prophets*. Ormsby describes the various vibrations supposedly emitted by bodies celestial and earthly. The phrase *good vibrations* was

popularized, however, by the rock band the Beach Boys in their 1966 hit single "Good Vibrations." Songwriter and Beach Boy Brian Wilson said he took lyrical inspiration from stories his mother would tell about picking up different vibes from different people.[10]

I like to caution people to consider the etymology of cultural slang words or phrases. To continue watching video teachings on YouTube or following your favorite Christian preachers and teachers on social media is fine and can help you to grow. However, you must become a proficient student of the Word who knows how to interpret Scripture. Jesus was a student of Scripture. The apostle Paul urged Timothy to follow that example: "Study to show yourself approved by God, a workman who need not be ashamed, rightly dividing the word of truth" (2 Timothy 2:15). I encourage you to invest in sound Bible study tools so you can also accomplish this.

Also, if you are reading Scripture but have incorrect interpretation, this can lead you into error and cause you to validate a supernatural encounter you experience that violates Scripture and should be rejected. Again, having "good vibes" or feeling "good energy" about something is not enough! Anything not connected to Scripture does not have life to produce manifestation and should be rejected.

Veiled Agendas

The manifestos of the Kingdom of God and the kingdom of darkness are revealed through culture. What constitutes culture has been identified in several different ways. The most popular description points to the "seven mountains of culture," designated as the mountains of education, government, media, arts and entertainment, marriage and family, finance/business, and religion/church. These are also referred to as seven cultural spheres of influence. I write about these spheres of influence in *Next-Level Believers*, but here, let me say that the manifesto of the Kingdom of God and the manifesto of the kingdom of darkness exist in these seven cultures in some measure. The role of believers, whom the Bible calls the Ekklesia, is to occupy by manifesting the Kingdom of God throughout every stratum of culture. The kingdom of darkness holds as its goal the same agenda.

The manifesto of the Kingdom of God does not operate covertly. In other words, our life of faith in Jesus Christ is available for all to access and experience. We are the light of the world (see Matthew 5:14). Jesus came that we might have the abundant life with Him. We access this Christ life through faith in Jesus Christ as our Redeemer.

The manifesto of the kingdom of darkness is also available for all to see and experience. One distinction from God's Kingdom is in the end result:

> But now, having been freed from sin and having become slaves of God, you have fruit unto holiness, and the end is eternal life. For the wages of sin is death, but the gift of God is eternal life through Jesus Christ our Lord.
>
> Romans 6:22–23

God offers abundant life, and Satan offers death. We tend to think in measurement terms: "a little rest," "a little food," etc. This translates into the way we perceive our level of righteousness: "a little lie," for example. The truth is that all lies are big, and they are not little or insignificant. This is how Satan veils his manifesto. We accept these perceptions as normal. Those who do not are labeled as "unbalanced, intolerant believers." I will say again, Satan veils his manifesto. He hides the consequences of alignment with him. He veils his deadly assignment in order to seduce people into acceptance.

The Snare of Compromise

We have been lulled into accepting unrighteousness as righteousness. We struggle to separate the profane from what is holy and righteous. We shrug off unrighteousness and label it as acceptable. Another way to see this is as leaven, which is a type of yeast. When yeast is placed inside dough, the dough rises. It does not remain the same size. As 1 Corinthians 5:6–7 says, "Do you not know that a little yeast leavens the whole batch? Therefore purge out the old yeast, that you may be a new batch." The acceptance of what you might consider small portions of unrighteousness leads to compromise and your acceptance of other issues.

Look at yoga as an example. We would all agree that exercise is a necessary activity. Stretching and toning our bodies and becoming physically fit has great impact on our physical and mental health. Yoga has become popular as a form of exercise, but let's look at yoga a bit more closely. *Charisma* magazine reported that Jean Nizza, a former psychic, made these comments during an interview with *CBN News* (on the Christian Broadcasting Network):

> Yoga is a Hindu spiritual practice, and the word 'yoga' is rooted in Sanskrit. It means 'to yoke to' or 'to unite with,' and what they're doing. . . . They have deliberate postures that are paying tribute, honor and worship to their false gods, and they have over 330,000,000 false gods, which are demons, and they're honoring them with these postures.[11]

This is an example of "a little leaven." Through the practice of yoga, Satan can introduce his deadly agenda. Nizza specifically spoke about Christians who use yoga to stay fit, explaining why she believes participating in this fitness phenomenon can be spiritually perilous. The article in *Charisma* continues:

> She called churches' embrace of yoga "heartbreaking," and said she, too, participated in the workout when she was a psychic and described how it became part of her daily mantra.
>
> "I used to do yoga ritualistically, and the meditation aspect really opened me up and helped me to receive communication from evil spirits," she said of her former psychic practices.

This is how, with just "a little leaven," we can find ourselves engaging in demonic encounters. Séances have also become popular over recent years. A séance is a meeting at which people attempt to make contact with the dead, especially through the agency of a medium. This phenomenon is not new. In ancient Israel, because of King Saul's repeated disobedience, God rejected him and announced through the prophet Samuel that He would establish David as king in Saul's place. After Samuel died, King Saul, who was in a war against the Philistines, sought the word of the Lord, but there was no response from the King of kings. God didn't respond because He had rejected Saul and His decision was final. King Saul then sought information from another source:

> Now Samuel died and all Israel mourned him, and they buried him in Ramah, his own city. And Saul had removed the mediums and the necromancers from the land.
>
> Then the Philistines gathered themselves together. And they came and camped in Shunem. So Saul gathered all Israel together, and they camped in Gilboa. When Saul saw the camp of the Philistines, he was afraid and his heart trembled

greatly. Saul inquired of the LORD, but the LORD did not answer him by dreams, or by lots, or by prophets. Then said Saul to his servants, "Seek for me a woman who is a medium, that I may go to her and inquire of her."

And his servants said to him, "There is woman medium in Endor."

So Saul disguised himself, put on other clothes, and he went with two of his men. And they came to the woman by night and he said, "Please divine for me by a spirit, and bring up for me whom I will name to you."

1 Samuel 28:3–8

When you experience encounters, you must discern the voice that is speaking. The most accurate way to do this is through the Word of God. Within the pages of Scripture, we discover truths concerning the character and nature of God and how He operates. Another way we can understand the operations of God can be seen in the word *patterns*. God is a God of process and patterns. He never violates His principles or patterns. He does not alter His eternal purposes. "Just as He chose us in Him before the foundation of the world, to be holy and blameless before Him in love; He predestined us to adoption as sons to Himself through Jesus Christ according to the good pleasure of His will" (Ephesians 1:4–5).

Discerning the Voice and Source

Another key to discerning the source of any encounter is the gift of discernment itself. The *Dictionary of Bible Imagery* tells us, "Discernment is an act of wisdom or detection marked by an insight into a person's character or by an event that comes through insight that goes beyond the facts given."[12] To discern simply means that you have a supernatural understanding of the voice that is speaking and the source.

Discernment is linked with prophetic accuracy. You can develop prophetic accuracy over time, and the key to unlocking this capacity is to understand how you perceive spiritual things. Many prophetic people are auditory. This means that they perceive prophetically through their hearing. During encounters, you are likely to hear things being spoken. You will also see things. You may experience sights and sounds that are not consistent with Scripture. Just as prophecy must be judged, encounters must be judged. In dream encounters, you might experience similitudes. You must not only discern and understand the activity, but also the spirit of the activity.

The greatest vision or encounter you can experience is a vision encounter with the Living Jesus. Yet having vision encounters is not a requirement to validate your salvation. We receive salvation through Christ, by faith. Some believers mistakenly perceive the purpose of vision encounters as a way to validate their salvation or spirituality. God has a different purpose for encounters. Encounters are purposed to reveal truth—biblical truth. Sound biblical doctrine must always take priority over encounters. As the apostle Paul urges,

> Preach the word, be ready in season and out of season, reprove, rebuke, and exhort, with all patience and teaching. For the time will come when people will not endure sound doctrine, but they will gather to themselves teachers in accordance with their own desires, having itching ears, and they will turn their ears away from the truth and turn to myths.
>
> 2 Timothy 4:2–4

I will repeat, God is a God of patterns and process. Encounters will profit you and then profit the Body of Christ.

Through discernment, we know the difference between good and evil: "But solid food belongs to those who are mature, for those who through practice have powers of discernment that are trained to distinguish good from evil" (Hebrews 5:14). We can see how discernment revealed to Paul the source of the voice speaking out of the servant girl in Acts 16:16–18:

> On one occasion, as we went to the place of prayer, a servant girl possessed with a spirit of divination met us, who brought her masters much profit by fortune-telling. She followed Paul and us, shouting, "These men are servants of the Most High God, who proclaim to us the way of salvation." She did this for many days. But becoming greatly troubled, Paul turned to the spirit and said, "I command you in the name of Jesus Christ to come out of her." And it came out at that moment.

This young girl was possessed by a spirit of divination. This is how the powers of darkness work to deceive human beings—through disguising themselves as ministers of righteousness. The Church must discern false encounters and false leadership, as did the Ephesian believers in Revelation 2:2. The Lord commended them, saying, "I know your works, your labor and your patience, and that you cannot bear those who are evil. And you have tested those who say they are apostles, but are not, and have found them to be liars."

A problem in the early Church was false doctrine. The apostle Paul had to contend with false teachers who would distort the pure message of the Gospel. He wrote to the Galatian church,

> I marvel that you are turning away so soon from Him who called you in the grace of Christ to a different gospel, which is not a gospel. But there are some who trouble you and would

pervert the gospel of Christ. Although if we or an angel from heaven preach any other gospel to you than the one we have preached to you, let him be accursed. As we said before, so I say now again: If anyone preaches any other gospel to you than the one you have received, let him be accursed.

Galatians 1:6–9

It is no different today. The principle of agreement requires any supernatural experience to be subjected to the Word of God and discarded if it does not agree with Scripture.

Encounters and Divination

In 2 Corinthians 11:13–15, Paul reveals why discernment is so vitally necessary for us as believers:

For such are false apostles and deceitful workers, disguising themselves as apostles of Christ. And no wonder! For even Satan disguises himself as an angel of light. Therefore it is no great thing if his ministers also disguise themselves as ministers of righteousness, whose end will be according to their works.

According to *Vine's Expository Dictionary of Biblical Words*, the meaning of *divination* is drawn from the word *puthon*, or *python*.[13] In Greek mythology, Puthon, or Python, was the name of the Pythian spirit or dragon that dwelled at the foot of Mount Parnassus, guarded the Oracle of Delphi, and was slain by Apollo. Thence the name was transferred to Apollo himself. Later, the word was applied to diviners or soothsayers, who were regarded as being inspired by Apollo. Demons are the agents inspiring idolatry (see 1 Corinthians 10:20).

Look again at the young woman Paul dealt with in Acts 16. She was possessed by a demon instigating the cult of Apollo, and thus she had a spirit of divination.[14] While what the young woman cried out was the truth, the incident was a demonic encounter. The spirit of divination was saying of Paul and the others, "These men are servants of the Most High God, who proclaim to us the way of salvation" (verse 17). While this was all true, these demonic spirits were attempting to align with the apostles so that their occult movement could gain legitimacy. The young servant girl was following the disciples daily and making the same declaration. This is a picture of how the spirit of mammon will partner with divination. This is also an example of why encounters must be interpreted through Scripture.

> **All spiritual activities must either be validated or rejected based on an accurate interpretation of Scripture. God never violates His Word.**

The Bible provides guidelines for encounters. All spiritual activities must either be validated or rejected based on an accurate interpretation of Scripture. God never violates His Word. Understanding the pattern of Scripture will therefore help you discern what kingdom operation you are being subjected to. We must understand Scripture's pattern. It is within the Word of God that we learn the ways and patterns of God.

Seeing Beyond

Beyond the earthly realm is where the supernatural realm operates. When you enter this supernatural realm, you have access to revelation given by the Spirit of God. Yet you must be aware of the fact that the powers of darkness are also speaking here. Again, this is the reason why discernment is a critical factor. Information from the supernatural realm is beyond information in the earthly realm. Only through Scripture can we know the source of something. The epistle of Jude speaks about fallen angels who possessed forbidden knowledge. These fallen angels still have the knowledge they had in heaven, and they will use it to ensnare human beings. Beware of demonic sources of information. Just because something is true doesn't mean it came from the Kingdom of God.

Not only that, but don't forget that when we prophesy, we touch supernatural realms. Whether given in the corporate setting or personally, prophecies should be judged (see 1 Corinthians 14:29). Satan attempts to come in with us unaware and create confusion and chaos through encounters with false prophecies. He delights in shifting your focus from God to anything else.

When you determine through Scripture and discernment that you have encountered the powers of darkness, you must cast them out, as Paul did in Acts 16:18: "She [the servant girl] did this for many days. But becoming greatly troubled, Paul turned to the spirit and said, 'I command you in the name of Jesus Christ to come out of her.' And it came out at that moment." Do not entertain conversations with demons.

The natural realm is host to the created order. Everything we see is part of this natural realm, and everything in it will sooner or later be gone. Only the supernatural realm endures forever. Heaven is part of the supernatural realm, as are angels. The kingdom of darkness is also part of the supernatural realm. There are moments in time where we can see both supernatural kingdoms operating in the earthly realm. Yet we often overlook the supernatural realm, as we tend to limit our thinking only to the natural realm. The supernatural realm opens up the prophetic realm, where we can perceive details about our future or issues that are on God's heart. Perhaps we think that only prophets can operate in this realm. Actually, God calls all believers to touch the prophetic realm. These are moments of encounters.

Early in my walk with the Lord, I learned to spend time in prayer. There came a period of time when I began to ask the Lord to take me to His throne room. Every day when I entered my place of prayer, I didn't end without spending time asking the Lord to take me there. I didn't know that I was asking for an encounter with Jesus. Weeks, maybe even months passed. I enjoyed incredible fellowship with the Lord during prayer. It was during one of these times that I felt a shift in the room. I didn't know it then, but I was in an encounter with heaven. The room was filled with light brighter than I had ever seen. It was as though I could hear the sounds of the stars. I had never before experienced such weighty glory. I was in a kneeling position when the weight of the Lord's presence just seemed to fall upon me. Although I didn't see His face, as John the apostle did, I understand why in John's encounter he fell as though he were dead (see Revelation 1:17).

I became aware that the reverential fear of God was filling me, and as it did, I began to weep uncontrollably. I didn't have language for the experience I was having. I started to wonder if I was getting ready to die. I asked myself, *Am I going to die in this prayer closet?* The thought filled my mind to the extent that I began to withdraw. My focus shifted from the amazing encounter that was unfolding, and then very quickly, the glory in the room dissipated. Whatever form an encounter takes, we need to keep our focus on God, who gives us such supernatural moments.

Encounters await each of us. God wants us to pursue Him in such a way that encounters unfold. Again, I caution you against seeking experiences more than seeking the author and finisher of our faith. We access this supernatural realm by faith. God is longing for deeper communication with His people. It's time to engage heaven in such a way that you experience daily downloads from God's heart through the door of God-encounters.

PRAYER ACTIVATION

I confess that I was created in the image and likeness of the Most High God, that I might encounter Him. I decree John 4:24 over my life, that I will worship Him in spirit and in truth. Lord, give me the desire to daily study Your Word, the Bible, so that I might know You in deeper ways. I activate my faith to believe that amazing experiences in the presence of the Most High God await me. In Jesus' name.

FIVE

Portals, Gates, and Doors

After this I looked. And there was an open door in heaven. The first voice I heard was like a trumpet speaking with me, saying, "Come up here, and I will show you things which must take place after this." Immediately I was in the Spirit.

Revelation 4:1–2

To further understand the realm of encounters, we must understand supernatural access points, which I will refer to as *portals*, *gates*, and *doors*. We often use these terms interchangeably. However, they carry the same meaning. They are entry points. How do we access this realm of encounters, and where is it? To help us find answers, let's look at two definitions on the subject.

In a *Charisma* magazine article, pastor and counselor Dr. Candice Smithyman provides this definition of supernatural access points: "Portals are described as doors, gateways or entrances to a place. From a spiritual perspective they are places that have been on earth from day one and we now have entrance to because of the death, burial, resurrection, and ascension of Jesus Christ."[1]

Vine's Expository Dictionary of Biblical Words translates the word *encounter* from *sumballo*, which means to throw together or "to make war against."[2] It is also translated as meeting in order to discuss. *Vine's* also uses the words *confer*, *help*, *ponder*, *meet*, or *make* in its definition.

From these definitions, we see that encounters convey the meaning of a meeting. We also see that these meetings can occur in various places. The names used to describe these places are doors, gateways, or entrances.

Another way to understand these places is through the term *access points*. These places provide access from the natural plane of existence into the spiritual plane. I believe there are places on earth that represent spiritual portals. These are places where there is an overwhelming sense of the presence of God. Here is one story of such a place from Scripture:

> Then Jacob went out from Beersheba and went toward Harran. He came to a certain place and stayed there all night, because the sun had set. He took one of the stones of that place and put it under his head, and lay down in that place to sleep. He dreamed and saw a ladder set up on the earth with the top of it reaching to heaven. The angels of God were ascending and descending on it. . . .
>
> Jacob awoke out of his sleep, and he said, "Surely the LORD is in this place, and I did not know it." He was afraid and said, "How awesome is this place! This is none other but the house of God, and this is the gate of heaven."
>
> Genesis 28:10–12, 16–17

Jacob had lain down to rest in a city called Luz. During the night, he experienced an encounter dream. He saw a ladder reaching from earth to heaven, and the angels of God were ascending and descending from it. Unknowingly, he had lain down in a place where a portal was operating. Now, it could be said that the portal opened because Jacob was there and God had planned this encounter with and for Jacob. Yet it could also be said that there was a portal of heaven open where Jacob lay down. This was a supernatural intersecting of heaven and earth, and Jacob was witness to heaven's activity. This is how portals can operate.

I believe there are places on earth that represent spiritual portals. These are places where there is an overwhelming sense of the presence of God.

In the same manner, we can also define a gate as a structural closure through a wall, a fence, or a barrier for the purpose of transitioning from one place to another. Gates allow people to move from one area into another. Like portals, they are access points that open the way into something. There are physical and spiritual gates, both of which are places of transition. I wrote this about gates in *Next-Level Believers*:

> Old Testament cities were surrounded by walls and gates. The benefits were that the gates provided protection and a place where government officials could meet to render judicial decisions (see Joshua 2:7; 2 Samuel 18:24; 19:8). The gates were also a place where business and social functions were carried out, where contracts were signed and witnessed, and where prophets could deliver the word of the Lord to the city elders (see Ruth 4:1; Jeremiah 7:1–3). Judicial verdicts were handed down at the gates. Absalom sat at the gate and stole the hearts of many of Israel's leaders from his father, King David (see 2 Samuel 15:2).

Gates were places of great strength. When Jesus declared that the gates of hell would not prevail against His Church, He was declaring that the forces of hell would not overcome the Church (see Matthew 16:18). Regardless of the plots, stratagems or strength of Satan and his angels, the Ekklesia will not be overcome. As the Ekklesia, we will face off the kingdom of Satan from generation to generation, but we will not be overcome.[3]

The manifesto of the Kingdom of God will prevail. "The kingdoms of the world have become the kingdoms of our Lord, and of His Christ, and He shall reign forever and ever" (Revelation 11:15).

I also wrote the following about gates in that same book:

Symbolic of authority and power, gates are mentioned numerous times throughout Scripture. Here are a few examples:

Go through, go through the gates. Prepare the way of the people; build up, build up the highway. Remove the stones; lift up a standard over the peoples (Isaiah 62:10).

Open the gates, that the righteous nation may enter, the one who remains faithful (Isaiah 26:2).

Therefore, your gates shall be open continually; they shall not be shut day nor night, so that men may bring to you the wealth of the nations, and that their kings may be brought (Isaiah 60:11).

Scripture also mentions examples like the *gate of heaven, Zion's gate,* and the *gates of righteousness:*

How awesome is this place! This is none other but the house of God, and this is the gate of heaven (Genesis 28:17).

The Lord loves the gates of Zion more than all the dwelling places of Jacob (Psalm 87:2).

Open to me the gates of righteousness; I will go into them, and I will praise the Lord (Psalm 118:19).

Then there are also *evil gates* that Scripture mentions:

I will go before you and make the crooked places straight; I will break in pieces the gates of bronze and shatter the bars of iron (Isaiah 45:2).

Thus says the Lord of Hosts: "The broad wall of Babylon will be utterly broken, and her high gates will be burned with fire; and the peoples will labor in vain, and the nations become exhausted only for fire" (Jeremiah 51:58).

I will build My church, and the gates of Hades shall not prevail against it (Matthew 16:18).

Following Peter's declaration that Jesus was the Christ, Son of the Living God, Jesus declared that the Church would be established on this truth: Christ is the Son of the Living God, and through Him we have redemption. *Clarke's Commentary* tells us that when Jesus went on to declare that He would build His Church and that the gates of hell would not overcome it, He was referring to the plots, stratagems and strength of Satan and his kingdom.

The Church has endured great persecution from generation to generation. Yet Jesus declared that the powers and stratagems of Satan's kingdom would not overcome the Church. In every generation, assignments of hell manifest against the Church, with a primary aim of silencing the Church. But the cornerstone of the Church is Christ Himself, who has already won the victory and who cannot be defeated. This is the truth the Church has been commissioned to declare and demonstrate—the power of Christ's supernatural Kingdom. It is important to remember that the Church is not the Kingdom of God. The Church is a manifestation of the Kingdom, and has been endued with power and authority to overcome the darkness.[4]

Encounter Testimony

Some years ago, I had an encounter dream. I was in a place unlike any place I had ever been. The technology was far beyond anything I had ever seen. A massive airport was in operation, or maybe more than one. Whenever a plane was taking off, which was often, the roof would open. I saw multitudes of helicopters in the sky above this place that looked as though it had no end. There were elevators going up that seemed unattached to the building. What was interesting is the fact that I didn't notice any planes or helicopters landing. Only departures. Neither were the elevators coming down; they were all going up. I wondered, *What is this place?*

Later in the dream, God gave me a message for myself alone that I have carried in my spirit ever since. The sounds were musical. The lights were almost translucent, and there was full sunlight. When I awakened, there was a weighty presence of God in the room. This was more than a dream experience; this was an encounter.

When we experience these moments, we are changed. The experience is somehow seared into our spirit. According to Dr. Candice Smithyman,

> We just need to know the keys or access points for entry. We enter these portals by faith. Faith comes through knowing the Word of God. You must wash in the Word to access heavenly portals and the eternal realm. The eternal realm is accessed by knowing what Jesus did from the Word of God and believing it.[5]

Dark Doors and Access Points

There are also access points to the demonic realm. One review of current movie listings and television programming informs us of an escalation of the kingdom of darkness into our homes through the access point called television. We are bombarded with images depicting lust, perversion, brutal violence, drug addiction, crime, etc. Through this gateway, demonic spirits are released into our homes.

During one of my travels, I had an opportunity to have dinner with an amazing intercessor. She has dedicated her life to dealing with demonic gateways that operate in the earth. God has deployed her to various nations to nullify through fasting, prayer, and intercession the demonic gateways operating in certain regions. She shared a testimony with me concerning many video games. During her employment with a major producer of video games, she was observing the production of the video files for games. It was during one of those observations that she saw a portal open through which demons were stepping into the files. With each layer, she saw a demon step into the game. When she went home at the end of her workday, she instructed her teenage son no longer to play video games.

On a later evening when her son returned home, she discerned that he had hidden a video game in his backpack, intending to play it despite her warning and instruction. He played it for several weeks. One evening, he went to his closet to retrieve an item, and standing in his closet was a demon. The video game had served as a gateway for demons to enter his domain. Startled, the young man asked, "Who are you, and why are you here?"

The demon replied, "I won't leave until *she* tells me I have to go," which this intercessor mother did.

I asked her why she had waited several weeks while her son played the game. She explained that the room was her son's domain. She had prayed in faith, asking the Lord to show him the demonic gateway operating through the video game. When her son saw the demonic in operation, he was willing to repent, which then gave this intercessor authority to command the demon to go.

Knowing the keys or access points to the demonic realm helps us know how demonic spirits are attempting to establish domains in our homes, ministries, or nations. In addition to movies, TV, and violent video games, here are some other things that create access points to the demonic realm: sin issues, unforgiveness, curses, familiar spirits, blood covenants, false worship, unyielded practices in our soul and flesh (including addictions), and occult activities like Ouija boards, séances, and such (see Galatians 5:19–21). Believers must become aware of these access points and live surrendered to the Holy Spirit.

Guard Your Gates

Your physical body has five gates: sight, hearing, touch, taste, and smell. More commonly, these five gates are called the senses, but they are also gates. They are access points. For example, when I am in the grocery store I often walk through the coffee aisle, which is usually pungent with the smell of coffee. Almost immediately, my desire awakens for a cup of coffee.

You can find commercials for different products in any form of media, whether print, social media, or television. By accessing your eye gates, these commercials are at work on you, attempting to influence you to buy certain products. Individuals who are bound by addictions such as pornography, drugs, or alcohol have been taken captive through their physical gates. In considering encounters, it is important to remember that in the supernatural realm, dark doors are also open. Satan looks for ways to access you through your senses, creating moments of demonic encounter.

I passed by one of these dark doors when I had the opportunity to travel to Washington, D.C., for a prayer journey. As I rode through the city, close to the area of several key government buildings, I started to feel sick. Waves of nausea began rising in me. Once we had driven beyond this particular area, the feeling of sickness lifted. I believe that a demonic portal was operating there. I'm not suggesting that all governmental operations or buildings are demonic. Many Christians are elected to office or serve their country in some way. Yet this particular spot we were passing through was an access point for the demonic.

Encounter Testimony

On another occasion, I was traveling to Indiana for prophetic training and activation. New to the prophetic at the time, I looked forward to the training. We had been driving for several hours and decided to stay at a motel since we were tired. It was a small property seemingly located in the middle of Nowhere, USA. When we arrived in our room I felt uncomfortable, but I didn't know why. We settled in, prepared for bed, and turned out the lights.

I soon drifted off to sleep, but not for long. I was somehow awakened. I hadn't heard a sound in the room, which was darker than any room I had ever slept in. I was tired and shouldn't have awakened, but here I was, awake. As I lay in the darkness, I looked up and suddenly saw a dark, shadowy spirit sitting on the closet rack, which was more like a metal coat rack. The shadowy figure leaped from the rack toward the bed where we were sleeping.

Even though it was dark because there was no natural illumination in the room, I could see the figure in the darkness. This was an encounter with a demon of fear and terror. The demon seemed to be moving in slow motion. As it came toward me, I actually stood up in the bed and began to say, "It's in here! Something is in here!"

I was sounding the alarm that evil was in the room. Later, as I processed the encounter, I began to sense that some previous guests who had occupied the room had prayed and released the spirit of divination. I also sensed that innocent blood had been shed in the room. We were new to the prophetic and to spiritual warfare, and we only knew one thing to do—leave! As we hurriedly left the motel, we were praying intensely. This was an encounter we had never had before.

Interestingly, when we arrived at the second hotel, I noticed that the spirit had followed us. I could sense the same dark presence. This time, I asked the Lord to send angels to watch over us. I asked the Lord to give me surrounding and covering angels, and He did. The demon's assignment was broken, and the demonic access was closed. You can cut off demonic access. The blood of Jesus protects us from darkness.

Error and Deception

Satan desires to lead you into error and deception. To accomplish this, he has programmed his arsenal of encounters. He masquerades as an "angel of light" and therefore attempts to bring you pseudo encounters. In these deceptive encounters, it is possible to hear voices telling you lies or distorted truth.

I knew someone who had had an encounter with the kingdom of darkness. A demon appeared to him and said, "If you follow me, I will make you rich."

This individual began to consider this possibility. He shared the encounter with several individuals at our church. Each of us who spoke to him about the matter warned him that this was not from God, but was rather a ploy of the enemy. He continued to consider the possibility that Satan would make him rich. We exposed the reality that Satan is the father of lies and that anything Satan had told him was not true.

Nonetheless, this individual backslid and began to serve the enemy. Not only did Satan not make him rich, but this person also committed a crime for which he spent several years in prison. Thankfully, he returned to faith in Christ at a later point in his life. This story shows why we need revelation from God.

Don't embark on a journey to discover new spiritual things so that you can appear more spiritual or have bragging rights about something you saw. Our motives must be pure. Satan will give you a guided tour into his realms and show you things designed to entrap you. He attempted the same thing with Jesus:

Then Jesus was led up into the wilderness by the Spirit to be tempted by the devil. And He had fasted for forty days and forty nights, and then He was hungry. And the tempter came to Him and said, "If You are the Son of God, command that these stones be turned into bread."

But He answered, "It is written, 'Man shall not live by bread alone, but by every word that proceeds out of the mouth of God.'"

Matthew 4:1–4

Avoid this trap that says, "I want to experience new spiritual encounters that no one has ever had before." If you position yourself in this way, you are at risk for error. I believe there are encounters that are incredible! Because the intent of encounters is to reveal God to us, I also believe that others may have had the same encounters. When you set about to create a mindset of exclusivity, however, you are at risk of shifting into error. Let your motive and focus be knowing our Lord and Savior Jesus Christ in deeper ways.

> Satan will give you a guided tour into his realms and show you things designed to entrap you. He attempted the same thing with Jesus.

Encounters are powerful and will either bring you into revelation truth that will strengthen your walk with the Lord, or they can bring you into error. One of these two things will occur.

Doors and Doorways

Doors and doorways represent places of transition. The *Dictionary of Bible Imagery* states, "The doorway, gate, portal or entryway is often associated with entrance into an area of great spiritual significance. . . . The door is one of the most significant parts of a house."[6] We can see an emphasis on doors, access, and transition in the following Scripture passages:

> Lift up your heads, O you gates; and be lifted up, you everlasting doors, that the King of glory may enter (Psalm 24:7).

> I am the door. If anyone enters through Me, he will be saved and will go in and out and find pasture (John 10:9).

> I know your works. Look! I have set before you an open door, and no one can shut it. For you have a little strength, and have kept My word, and have not denied My name (Revelation 3:8).

> Listen! I stand at the door and knock. If anyone hears My voice and opens the door, I will come in and dine with him, and he with Me (Revelation 3:20).

> When they arrived and had assembled the church, they reported what God had done through them and how He had opened the door of faith to the Gentiles (Acts 14:27).

Doors reveal places of access and transition. Closed doors are a picture of lack of access. John the apostle, the writer of the book of Revelation, writes concerning an encounter he experienced: "After this I looked. And there was an open door in heaven" (Revelation 4:1). John saw a door opened in heaven. In other words, he was given access to ascend through a heavenly door that had opened. It is important to note that in Revelation 1:10 John states, "I was in the Spirit on the Lord's Day, and I heard behind me a great voice like a trumpet." We can conclude here that John was already in a spiritual realm, which facilitated a vision of and revelation for the seven churches of Asia (see Revelation 1:12–16). Yet in Revelation 4:1, John is instructed, "Come up here." He was being invited to ascend into a higher, yet deeper level of revelation. He was being invited to go through the door.

This is the nature of encounters. They are an invitation to us to ascend beyond where we have been and come up into the next level with God.

Into the Deep

The kingdom of darkness is as real as the Kingdom of God. Human beings can gain access to both kingdoms. Access to God's Kingdom and plans requires faith: "And without faith it is impossible to please God, for he who comes to God must believe that He exists and that He is a rewarder of those who diligently seek Him" (Hebrews 11:6). Faith is the key to occupying the realm of God-encounters. Knowing that we were created for fellowship with our Creator, placing priority on pursuing a relationship with Him above supernatural experiences, and trusting that what He has in mind for us is good, will unlock this realm. I call this measure of pursuit "the deep place." It is where we begin to experience the extraordinary because we are willing to go beyond.

Luke 5:4 states about Jesus, "When He had finished speaking, He said to Simon, 'Launch out into the deep and let down your nets for a catch.'" This deep is a realm you must contend for. Too many believers are content to live in shallow places in the Spirit. They are much like the Laodicean Church, about which the Lord said,

I know your works, that you are neither cold nor hot. I wish you were cold or hot. So then, because you are lukewarm, and neither cold nor hot, I will spit you out of My mouth. For you say, "I am rich, and have stored up goods, and have need of nothing," yet do not realize that you are wretched, miserable, poor, blind, and naked.

Revelation 3:15–17

These Laodicean believers were indifferent. *Clarke's Commentary* states of them,

> They were listless and indifferent, and seemed to care little whether heathenism or Christianity prevailed. Though they felt little zeal either for the salvation of their own souls or that of others, yet they had such a general conviction of the truth and importance of Christianity, that they could not readily give it up.[7]

Those in the Laodicean Church were not unlike many believers in today's churches. Today, widespread indifference to spiritual things has halted the pursuit of God and spiritual things.

Perhaps you are one of those who struggles to pursue the "deep things of God." Spiritual encounters are deep things. I invite you to pray this prayer with me: *"Lord, I ask that you rekindle the fire and passion of the Kingdom of God in me again. Let the blood of Jesus quicken everything that is dead within me. In Jesus' name."*[8] Be encouraged to know that when you pray, God listens. He is committed to you and your walk with Him.

Waiting Deeply

When you arise in faith to believe that God-encounters are not only for those we deem "super spiritual," but are moments available for all believers, you will begin to experience incredible moments with the Lord. Your time in prayer will be filled with expectation and wonderment concerning what the Lord will say and do.

Waiting isn't always easy, but the Lord rewards us for our waiting. He gives power to the faint, and He increases strength in those who have no might:

> Even the youths shall faint and be weary, and the young men shall utterly fall, but those who wait upon the LORD shall renew their strength; they shall mount up with wings as eagles, they shall run and not be weary, and they shall walk and not faint.
>
> Isaiah 40:30–31

Learning to wait deeply upon the Lord is where encounters occur. We are not prepared to wait in this way. We want everything now. Our lives are hurried and rushed. We are primed for instant gratification. Yet the realm of encounters is a waiting realm. It is not hurried or rushed. There is not a sense of time there. Time is relevant to the earth.

When you begin to engage in the realm of encounters, some of the amazing benefits that await you are *refreshing (joy)*, *renewal (strength)*, *revelation (sight)*, *restoration (of loss)*, and *revival (purpose)*. Let's look at each of these more closely for a moment, along with some Scriptures about them. I encourage you to include these Scripture references in your prayer time and watch amazing things unfold.

Refreshing (Joy)

Joy is different from happiness. Happiness can be momentary, but refreshing joy is a fruit of the Spirit that is cultivated in our lives over time. As we develop in our faith walk, the Spirit helps us overcome adversities. This produces the fruit of joy.

Do not be grieved, for the joy of the LORD is your strength (Nehemiah 8:10).

For you, O LORD, have made me glad through Your work; I will sing joyfully at the works of Your hands (Psalm 92:4).

The meek also shall increase their joy in the LORD, and the poor among men shall rejoice in the Holy One of Israel (Isaiah 29:19).

Therefore, the redeemed of the LORD shall return and come with singing to Zion, and everlasting joy shall be upon their head. They shall obtain gladness and joy, and sorrow and mourning shall flee away (Isaiah 51:11).

Renewal (Strength)

Strength is linked with ability. You must develop a dependency on the Lord not only to help you through circumstances, but also to give you supernatural capacity to wait deeply on Him. Renewal means to make new again. In this instance, your strength is made new.

He gives power to the faint, and to those who have no might He increases strength (Isaiah 40:29).

It is God who clothes me with strength, and gives my way integrity (Psalm 18:32).

Let the words of my mouth and the meditation of my heart be acceptable in Your sight, O LORD, my strength and my Redeemer (Psalm 19:14).

May He send you help from the sanctuary, and strengthen you from Zion (Psalm 20:2).

That you may walk in a manner worthy of the Lord, pleasing to all, being fruitful in every good work, and increasing in the knowledge of God, strengthened with all might according to His glorious power, enduring everything with perseverance and patience joyfully (Colossians 1:10–11).

Revelation (*Sight*)

The realm of encounters is a place of revelation. God not only shows us His plan; He reveals our place in His plan. Without an understanding of His plan and our place in the plan of heaven, we can miss our assignment.

The LORD has made known His salvation; His righteousness He has revealed in the sight of the nations (Psalm 98:2).

Thus says the LORD: Preserve justice and do righteousness, for My salvation is about to come and My righteousness to be revealed (Isaiah 56:1).

He reveals the deep and secret things; He knows what is in the darkness, and the light dwells with Him (Daniel 2:22).

The One who forms the mountains and creates the wind, who reveals His thoughts to man, who turns the darkness into dawn and strides on the heights of the earth—the LORD, the God of Hosts, is His name (Amos 4:13).

To reveal for all people what is the fellowship of the mystery, which from the beginning of the ages has been hidden in God, who created all things through Jesus Christ (Ephesians 3:9).

Restoration (of Loss)

Deeply waiting in the Lord's presence unlocks restoration. Unhealed issues creating a spirit of loss and trauma are restored during encounters. We must move in our Kingdom assignment from a place of wholeness. Let the Lord deal with any issues of loss and trauma that might be plaguing you.

He restores my soul; He leads me in paths of righteousness for His name's sake (Psalm 23:3).

Restore to me the joy of Your salvation, and uphold me with Your willing spirit (Psalm 51:12).

Restore us to Yourself, O Lord, that we may return! Renew our days as of old (Lamentations 5:21).

But after you have suffered a little while, the God of all grace, who has called us to His eternal glory through Christ Jesus, will restore, support, strengthen, and establish you (1 Peter 5:10).

Revival (Purpose)

Revival is part of renewal. When this occurs, we are restored to the purposes of the Lord. Our strength returns, and a vision for our future is unlocked.

The counsel of the LORD stands forever, the purposes of His heart to all generations (Psalm 33:11).

Will You not revive us again, that Your people may rejoice in You? (Psalm 85:6).

To everything there is a season, a time for every purpose under heaven (Ecclesiastes 3:1).

For thus says the High and Lofty One who inhabits eternity, whose name is Holy: I dwell in the high and holy place and also with him who is of a contrite and humble spirit, to revive the spirit of the humble, and to revive the heart of the contrite ones (Isaiah 57:15).

We know that all things work together for good to those who love God, to those who are called according to His purpose (Romans 8:28).

The Bible provides the foundation for God-encounters. These are not simply hyper-spiritual moments. God is revealing something relevant to your life and purpose in them. It is time to overcome frustration and discouragement. Take a step of faith and believe that encounters with God await you.

PRAYER ACTIVATION

I decree today that the horn of God's salvation is pouring out anointing upon me. I plead the blood of Jesus against every evil spirit keeping me in a low place. Lord, today I am rising in a new way to walk through portals of heaven that You desire to open to me. My life is soaked with anointing today.[9] Thank You for teaching me how to wait deeply upon You.

SIX

Presence Driven

And He said, "My Presence will go with you, and I will give you rest." Then he said to Him, "If Your Presence does not go with us, do not bring us up from here."

Exodus 33:14–15

We have established the biblical foundation for supernatural encounters with the Living God, who is the author and initiator of these moments with us. Our approach to God must be predicated on faith. We are to seek the righteousness of God's Kingdom every day and in every area of life. Our priority must be His will.

Matthew 6:33 (TPT) states, "So above all, constantly seek God's kingdom and his righteousness, then all these less important things will be given to you abundantly." Our priority must shift from being experience driven to becoming presence driven. Could becoming presence driven, and then understanding how to continually host God's presence, be a key to seeing great miracles, signs, and wonders manifested in our corporate gatherings?

Being presence driven extends beyond experiencing periodic Holy Ghost goose bumps. What I am describing here is the breathtaking majesty and power of the King of all kings, the Supreme Ruler of the universe. This is what Isaiah encountered in Isaiah 6:1–5:

> I saw the Lord sitting on a throne, high and lifted up, and His train filled the temple. Above it stood the seraphim. . . . One cried to another and said:
>
> > "Holy, holy, holy, is the LORD of Hosts;
> > the whole earth is full of His glory."
>
> The posts of the door moved at the voice of him who cried, and the house was filled with smoke.
> And I said: "Woe is me! For I am undone because I am a man of unclean lips, and I dwell in the midst of a people of unclean lips. For my eyes have seen the King, the LORD of Hosts."

This was a moment of commissioning. Isaiah was being commissioned as a prophet to carry the word of the Lord to the nation of Israel. What an amazing commissioning.

Encounters can include divine instructions concerning your life and destiny. Isaiah was being sent to a nation given to continual backsliding. True to His manifesto, God loved this nation and continued to pursue fellowship with its people. We can see His intent in 2 Peter 3:9: "He is patient with us, because He does not want any to perish, but all to come to repentance." God desires fellowship with us. We must desire His presence more than anything else. True hunger for His presence will drive you to His presence.

"Blessed are those who hunger and thirst for righteousness, for they shall be filled" (Matthew 5:6). Hunger is powerful and must be satisfied. Esau sold his birthright because he was hungry (see Genesis 25:29–34). True hunger is a driving force that longs for satisfaction. Likewise, when we truly hunger for God, we dare not accept any substitutes. True hunger for God's presence will drive us to spend time with Him. Only His presence will satisfy: "For He satisfies the longing soul and fills the hungry soul with goodness" (Psalm 107:9).

> **True hunger for God's presence will drive us to spend time with Him. Only His presence will satisfy.**

God's Manifest Presence

One effect of a God-encounter is presence—the presence of God. In his book *The God Chasers*, author Tommy Tenney makes a distinction between the omnipresence of God and the manifest presence of God. The omnipresence of God means that He is everywhere at the same time. There is no place where God is not. King David sang about this fact in Psalm 139:7–10:

> Where shall I go from Your spirit, or where shall I flee from Your presence? If I ascend to heaven, You are there; if I make my bed in Sheol, You are there. If I take the wings of the morning and dwell at the end of the sea, even there Your hand shall guide me, and Your right hand shall take hold of me.

This is a picture of the omnipresence of God, which is different from His manifest presence. As Tenney puts it in his book, "The manifested presence of God is moments when God concentrates or reveals Himself more strongly in one place than another."[1]

Encounters are markedly different from the omnipresence of God. We can sense God, and by faith we know He is everywhere at the same time, but we are not experiencing the weightiness of His presence at all times. We experience the weight when He manifests His presence in an encounter.

It is not unusual even to lose track of time and place during an encounter with God. The supernatural realm does not operate in the same way the earthly realm operates. The laws of time and distance do not apply. The apostle Paul was unable to determine whether he was in or out of his body during a particular encounter:

> Although it may not accomplish a thing, I need to move on and boast about supernatural visions and revelations of the Lord. Someone I'm acquainted with, who is in union with Christ, was swept away fourteen years ago in an ecstatic experience. He was taken into the third heaven, but I'm not sure if he was in his body or out of his body—only God knows. And I know that this man (again, I'm not sure if he was still in his body or taken out of his body—God knows) was caught up in an ecstatic experience and brought into paradise, where he overheard many wondrous and inexpressible secrets that were so sacred that no mortal is permitted to repeat them.
>
> 2 Corinthians 12:1–4 TPT

God is a God of patterns and process. During God-encounters there is an incredible weight of His glory present. These moments, which can actually be timeless places, build our faith and strengthen our conviction. This is a picture of how God's patterns and processes operate.

The Principle of Agreement

The realm of the Holy Spirit is a realm of order. There are spiritual principles that govern this realm. You cannot violate spiritual principles. An important factor that must govern and establish the validity of any encounter is what I call "the principle of agreement." This principle says that *any encounter that does not agree with the Word of God must be discarded as being false.*

In our consideration of supernatural encounters, we must take into account the importance of "agreement." I have known believers who have reported supernatural encounters that are in direct conflict with the Word of God. In other words, there was no agreement between their experience and the Bible. According to the principle of agreement, those encounters needed to be discarded.

Another word that will help us understand agreement is *harmony.* To be in harmony, or to be harmonious, means to have an agreement of the heart, desires, and wishes. Very little can be accomplished outside harmony. The purpose of God-encounters is to reveal some aspect of God and His plans for us. When we come into agreement with God and His Word concerning presenting ourselves spirit, soul, and body to Him, we are positioning ourselves for supernatural encounters.

Heaven's intent in encounters is not for the purpose of providing mere information or entertainment. The intent is revelational, so that we gain prophetic understanding of God's truth. It is the truth that we know that brings forth understanding. During times of supernatural encounter,

God reveals truth. Jesus said, "If you remain in My word, then you are truly My disciples. You shall know the truth, and the truth shall set you free" (John 8:31–32). There is no certainty to truth we are unsure of. Wherever uncertainty exists, there is confusion. Encounters reveal truth.

I have known believers who have reported having supernatural experiences where, as I watched the aftermath, I could tell that a spirit of deception had captured them. One individual began to preach that he himself was Jesus. This is why encounters must be interpreted through Scripture. When an experience does not honor God, it didn't come from God. If the experience does not lead you to Jesus, who is truth, it is leading you somewhere else—and the only other option is darkness and deception.

I want to share a prophecy with you about dispelling deception. I heard the Spirit of God say this: *For this is a time and a season that you will intimately know truth. For I have come to dispel lies and deceptions that have held you captive in religious traditions of men. I am even increasing discernment within you. You will discern and know what is true and what is false. You will discern the holy from that which is profane. For I, the Lord, will have you established in truth, which leads to righteousness.*

Jesus prayed for believers to be established in truth. This leads to unshakable faith concerning God and His purposes. As He told us in John 14:16–18,

> I will pray the Father, and He will give you another Counselor, that He may be with you forever: the Spirit of truth, whom the world cannot receive, for it does not see Him, neither does it know Him. But you know Him, for He lives with you, and will be in you. I will not leave you fatherless. I will come to you.

It is not enough to be acquainted with or familiar with the truth. We must learn to walk in the truth. Truth is linked with freedom. It sustains freedom. Many people are held captive by lies. Wherever you have believed a lie, you are held captive in that area. You will not be able to move beyond the limitations of the lie until you embrace the power of God's Word. Declare this right now: *I am no longer held captive by the lies and deceits of the enemy. It is the truth I know that makes me free. Beginning today, I commit myself to studying the Word of God and to embracing the truth He shows me!*

Now, shout *"TRUTH!"*

Encountering the *Logos*

Every believer needs to encounter the God of the Bible. His manifesto is outlined there. Encounters in the Word of God move you from reading to revelation. Revelation is connected to encounters. The *Dictionary of Biblical Imagery* explains it this way:

> What is the meaning of the biblical motif of the divine – human encounter? Above all, it is the paradigm of the Bible's view of reality, the heart of which is that God communicates to people and enters their lives providentially and redemptively as well as in judgment. People are not left as orphans in the universe. They are instead the recipients of a divine word and of divine provision for their earthly and eternal needs. In addition to the specific narrative archetype of the divine – human encounter, the Bible itself possesses the quality of an encounter. Its claim upon his readers to respond is coercive in a way that ordinary literature is not. The Bible presupposes response as a condition of reading it.[2]

Encounters must be interpreted through the lens of Scripture, not through a supernatural experience. Without validation from the Word of God, you are at risk of becoming unbalanced and spiritually spooky. Being imbalanced creates error and deception. God's Word tells us how He does and does not operate. When people have experienced deception, it is through the light of Scripture that they are able to identify that deception has taken place.

In the same way that God-encounters create conviction, demonic encounters can also create conviction. You might believe that because you experienced something, it must be the Spirit of God. Don't interpret your experiences by experiences; interpret and validate every experience through the Word of God. The Word reveals God's character. Satan will attempt to provide you with false information so he can affect your outcome. However, our system of defense against error and deception is the Word. We must ask ourselves questions like, *What does the Bible say about this kind of experience?*

Powerless Living

Encounters should manifest in the life of every believer. Understand that the Lord has constructed the encounters everyone will need for their entire life on earth. We simply need to get into position and walk through the door. A lack of encounters creates limitations in our walk with God. These supernatural moments bring assurance and conviction to our lives that God is real, and that He is invested in us. Encounters are moments of reality checks. When you have had an encounter, it changes your perception of reality.

I have had seasoned believers confess to wondering whether God even hears their prayers. This is evidence of the lack of encounters. When we have these encounter experiences, they bring reality and conviction to us because they establish the reality of God in our lives. In reality, encounters strengthen our convictions. The fact of experiencing something beyond our normal understanding informs our thinking in that area. Many believers are unstable in their walk with Christ due to the lack of encounters with Him. Having only superficial knowledge of God diminishes our faith in who He is and in His plans for us. We can find ourselves halted between opinions, which is double-mindedness. Here's what the Bible says about double-mindedness:

A double-minded man is unstable in all his ways (James 1:8).

Draw near to God, and He will draw near to you. Cleanse your hands, you sinners, and purify your hearts, you double-minded (James 4:8).

When we are double-minded, we have no clear conviction. Encounters create conviction, which leads us to faith. Faith is the essential element that must be developed in the life of every believer. God-encounters create moments during which encounters and conviction intersect, resulting in the enlargement of our faith.

> God-encounters create moments during which encounters and conviction intersect, resulting in the enlargement of our faith.

What I am trying to establish here is that the more encounters we have, the more our faith increases. I recognize that this premise will challenge the way in which you personally view encounters. Is it possible, however, that the Lord led you to read this book to bring you into a new understanding of encounters with Him? I pray that this book will create a new hunger within you to know the God of encounters in a deeper way.

The Encounter Generation

Another issue I want to raise here concerns the Millennial and Z generations. I believe they are hungry to know Jesus. I believe their hearts cry out in the same way as the apostle Paul's:

> . . . that I may gain Christ, and be found in Him, not having my own righteousness which is from the law, but that which is through faith in Christ, the righteousness which is of God on the basis of faith, to know Him, and the power of His resurrection, and the fellowship of His sufferings, being conformed to His death.
>
> Philippians 3:8–10

I am convinced that the Millennial and Z generations are destined for great Kingdom impact. This is why the manifesto of darkness has escalated the attacks against them through rebellion against authority, drug addiction, immorality, identity confusion, witchcraft and the occult, and a host of other demonically inspired issues. Yet beyond all of this, there is in these generations a desire to know God. Religious gatherings lacking the anointing will not appeal to them. They want to "know" Him.

I want to share another prophecy the Spirit of the Lord gave me: *For surely My hand is upon the Millennial and Z generations. The anointing of the revivalist is upon them. The intensity in which they have served the manifesto of darkness is not to be compared to the intensity in which they will serve My manifesto. They carry My revival move. Even now, I am brooding over them, and My word has gone forth concerning them. I remind you of My Word that says, "I will say to the north, 'Give them up,' and to the south, 'Do not keep them back. Bring My sons from afar, and My daughters from the ends of the earth.'" For you are My Encounter Generation! You will encounter Me again and again, and as you do, My glory will be released through you. I say to the Millennial and Z generations, you are Mine.*

God has declared Himself as the God of Abraham, Isaac, and Jacob. This helps us understand the intergenerational nature of God. He looks for worshipers in every generation. Our corporate gatherings must reflect multiple generations moving together carrying the agenda of heaven. Looking at the current landscape of churches, we can readily see the disengagement of the Millennial and Z generations. They are not interested in religious rhetoric or formality. Their desire is to experience the raw power of God! Not only must we contend for a generation, but we must also contend for Kingdom power that comes as the result of encounters with God.

Grace to Contend

Encounters come as the result of the pursuit to know God and His ways. These occurrences create conviction, which enlarges our faith. It's not the experiences that we should pursue, but the presence of God. To know Him must be our constant desire.

Unless you become willing to contend for a life of encounters with the Living God, you will not experience these moments. In fact, it is possible to miss them altogether. The apostle Paul urged his spiritual son, Timothy, to contend for the faith (see 1 Timothy 1:18; Jude 1:3). According to *Vine's Expository Dictionary of Biblical Words*, to *contend* refers to contending about a thing as a combatant, as in contest.[3] To *contend* is a warfare term. We are in a war against darkness. In this war, Jesus has won the victory:

> He blotted out the handwriting of ordinances that was against us and contrary to us, and He took it out of the way, nailing it to the cross. And having disarmed authorities and powers, He made a show of them openly, triumphing over them by the cross.
>
> Colossians 2:14–15

We must enforce the victories of Christ. Encounters with the Living God help us contend in the power of the Spirit until we overcome. The kingdom of darkness never takes a vacation; therefore, we must be vigilant in watching for the subtle ways in which darkness attacks. I am not telling you to go looking for a demon under every bush or behind every door. What I am saying is the devil is relentless in his pursuit to defeat us. We must be even more relentless in contending for the faith.

Purified for Influence

When considering encounters, which are an invitation from the Lord Jesus to know Him, we must consider our motives. Our desire for supernatural encounters with God must be motivated by the desire to know Him and bring Him glory. Supernatural encounters increase our influence. These amazing moments shift us from mediocre spiritual lives to becoming believers filled with conviction, which leads to faith and influence. In my book *Next-Level Believers*, I define *influence* as "the capacity or power of persons or things to be a compelling force on or produce effects on the actions, behaviors, opinions, etc., of others."[4] Encounters with God increase your influence, as you are not limited to speaking theoretically about deeper matters of the Spirit. Rather, after encounters you can now speak experientially, which adds the weight of conviction and glory to your words.

I have known and studied the lives of people who have amazing testimonies of supernatural encounters with Jesus, and I have noted a common thread—humility. Don't allow pride to enter your life and cause you to boast about your experiences. We must never seek to glorify ourselves. All glory and honor belong to the Lord Jesus. Humility will help you maintain balance. Without balance, you can go into error.

Encounters are not an earthly manifestation. They are spiritual events that affect our earthly life of faith. We all face challenges designed to divert us from our destiny and assignment. It is therefore critical for us to experience supernatural God-encounters. Continuity in our walk of destiny requires such encounters. Encounters supply the stability and fortitude we need. We become stronger; our conviction and faith increase. It is then that our influence for the Kingdom enlarges, and we begin to experience great results in life and ministry. This is what influence looks like.

> Encounters are not an earthly manifestation. They are spiritual events that affect our earthly life of faith.

Encounters reveal Christ in us. We can see who we are in Him and why He has created us. They are the indication that we have been spending time in the presence of God. Perhaps you have a desire to go deeper in the things of the Spirit. You may be wondering how to host the presence of God. Here are some practical strategies to move you from mediocrity in the Spirit to becoming a believer whose life is marked by the weighty presence of God.

1. *Develop the practice of consistent study of the Word of God.* The Word of God is living bread, vital to our spiritual health and development. If you lack knowledge of the Bible, by default you will lack the capacity to interpret God-encounters. There is no higher authority for our lives than God's Word. If you lack biblical understanding, you cannot understand the plans and intentions of God (see Psalm 25; 78:1; 2 Timothy 2:15; 3:16).

2. *Develop a consistent life of fellowship with the Holy Spirit.* We have the indwelling of the Holy Spirit, who teaches us all things and reveals Jesus to us. Through the Holy Spirit we can develop powerful lives of prayer and worship, thereby creating the necessary foundation for encounters (see Psalm 119:66; 143:10; John 14:26).

3. *Develop a desire for the supernatural.* With Jesus our Lord and Redeemer as the focus of your encounters, seek revelation that He desires to show you. Ask the Lord for grace to contend for supernatural manifestations. Ask the Lord to help you not miss the encounters He is sending you (see Romans 12:6–8; 1 Corinthians 12; 14).

4. *Develop a consistent pattern of fasting.* When you study the ministry of Jesus, you will see that He fasted often, as did the apostles of the early Church. Believers should commit to a life of fasting at least one day per week. If you haven't fasted for a while,

try water fasting until noon. After a few of these half-day fasts, increase your time to 3:00 p.m. Drink plenty of water. Over time, you can increase your fasting to overnight. During your fast, pray as much as possible. Fasting must include prayer to be classified as a fast (see Isaiah 58; Psalm 109:24; Matthew 6:17; Mark 2:18; Acts 13:3).

5. *Don't forget what God shows you.* I recommend journaling. Keep a journal of the things you encounter in the supernatural realm. As you review your journal entries, over time you will see the consistent messages God is speaking to you (see Psalm 42:4; 63:6; 77:11; Ecclesiastes 12:10; Revelation 1:19).

PRAYER ACTIVATION

Lord, I thank You that I was created to experience encounters with You. Help me live each day in Your presence. I rebuke every assignment of defeat, infirmity, demotion, demonic delay, confusion, backward movement, failure to progress further, and any other assignment of hell attempting to block my forward movement.[5] Today, I receive grace to contend, in Jesus' name.

SEVEN

Fire on the Altar

I urge you therefore, brothers, by the mercies of God, that you present your bodies as a living sacrifice, holy, and acceptable to God, which is your reasonable service of worship.

Romans 12:1

The altar is a vital component of our relationship with Christ. We are commanded to present our bodies as a living sacrifice, holy, and acceptable to God, which is our reasonable service of worship. The life of a believer is a sacrificial life. Jesus told His disciples, "If anyone will come after Me, let him deny himself, and take up his cross, and follow Me" (Matthew 16:24). This is the first component of our life in God's Kingdom. When we receive Him, we begin a life of sacrifice. This is also when we establish the altar of God in our lives. The altar is where the sacrifice lives.

The activity of sacrificing on the altar is what gives the altar life and meaning. In their book *Rekindle the Altar Fire*, Chuck Pierce and Alemu Beeftu write, "Without the altar there is no place for the sacrifice, and without the sacrifice there is no fire.

The fire of God consumes the sacrifice. Without the fire of His presence there is no glory."[1] Without continual sacrifice, the altar can fall into disrepair. They also write, "An altar cannot be blown down by the wind; it can only be torn down by our own hands. If we forget the altars, if we're tired of them, if we move on from them, the stones slowly crumble. But if we return, if we remember, if we stand firm, the stones remain."[2]

Your spiritual development requires you to build and maintain the altar. Nothing in our spiritual lives is accidental. Your growth and development require daily commitment. When you are intentional about seeking God, He will respond. This is when encounters occur. The altar is where encounters are initiated. Pierce and Beeftu go on,

> Without the altar of God signifying the cross, there is no life, no hope and no spiritual blessing. All of our spiritual needs can be met only through the work of the cross. That is why the word of God calls us to approach the throne of grace with confidence, so that we may receive mercy and find grace. . . . The altar is where we understand the depth of His love, His eternal purposes and His destiny for our lives. The altar is where we receive daily victory.[3]

According to the *Dictionary of Biblical Imagery*, the most prominent biblical image for worship and religious allegiance is an altar. In the Old Covenant, building altars and traveling to them to make sacrifices and offerings was the most visible sign of devotion to the true God.[4]

Finally, Pierce and Beeftu add about the word *altar*,

> The word altar comes from a verb that means literally, "to slaughter." A dictionary definition elaborates: "an elevated place or structure . . . at which religious rites are performed

or on which sacrifices are offered to gods, ancestors, etc." Furthermore, the word altar is used in Hebrews 13:10 for the sacrifice offered upon it, the sacrifice Christ offered.[5]

The Matter of Altars

Throughout Scripture, the word *altar* appears 368 times in the Modern English Version of the Bible. We first find the word *altar* in the Old Testament. Described as a raised platform, the altar was a place of sacrifice unto the Most High God. Genesis 4:3–4 gives the account of Cain and Abel offering a sacrifice to God. Although we can conclude from this account that an altar was built, we first find the word *altar* in Genesis 8:20, in reference to Noah. After emerging from the ark, Noah built an altar and offered God a sacrifice. The subject of altars is important throughout Scripture. Here are several examples to help you engage in your own study of this important topic.

Holy Altars

The LORD appeared to Abram and said, "To your descendants I will give this land." So he built an altar to the LORD, who had appeared to him. From there he continued on to a mountain to the east of Bethel and pitched his tent, having Bethel on the west and Ai on the east. There he built an altar to the LORD and called on the name of the LORD (Genesis 12:7–8).

Then Solomon stood in front of the altar of the LORD in the presence of all the congregation of Israel and spread his hands toward heaven (1 Kings 8:22).

Then I will go to the altar of God, to the God of my joyful gladness; with the harp I will give thanks to You, O God, my God (Psalm 43:4).

Therefore, when He came into the world, He said: "Sacrifices and offerings You did not desire, but a body You have prepared for Me. In burnt offerings and sacrifices for sin You have had no pleasure. Then I said, 'See, I have come to do Your will, O God,' as it is written of Me in the volume of the book" (Hebrews 10:5–7).

Another angel, having a golden censer, came and stood at the altar. He was given much incense to offer with the prayers of all the saints on the golden altar which was before the throne (Revelation 8:3).

Evil Altars

But this is how you shall deal with them: You shall destroy their altars and break down their images and cut down their Asherim and burn their graven images with fire (Deuteronomy 7:5).

And you shall overthrow their altars, and break their pillars, and burn their Asherah poles with fire, and you shall cut down the engraved images of their gods, and eliminate their names out of that place (Deuteronomy 12:3).

You must not make a pact with the inhabitants of this land, and you must tear down their altars (Judges 2:2).

Then Gideon built an altar for the LORD there and called it The LORD Is Peace. Even to this day it stands in Ophrah of the Abiezrites.

That night the LORD said to him, "Take a bull from your father's herd and a second bull seven years old. Tear down your father's Baal altar and cut down the Asherah pole beside it. Then build an altar to the LORD your God on top of this stronghold in an orderly way. Take the second bull and offer it as a burnt offering with the wood of the Asherah pole that you will cut down" (Judges 6:24–26).

When the king of Moab saw that the battle was overwhelming him, he took with him seven hundred swordsmen to break through to the king of Edom, but they were unable. Then he took his firstborn son, who would have reigned in his place, and offered him for a burnt offering on the wall. And great wrath came upon Israel, and they departed from him and returned to their own land (2 Kings 3:26–27).

We can see from Scripture that in the beginning, altars were established to worship and honor the Living God. Later in Scripture, we can see how Satan initiated altars for worship unto himself. Evil altars are established through patterns of sin and disobedience to God. When you say no to God in any area, by default you are saying yes to evil. Repeated rejection of God's ways of righteousness creates thrones of iniquity powered by evil altars. There were many false altars surrounding ancient Israel. Pagan worship included child sacrifice. I believe that abortion, the shedding of innocent blood, is a continuance of pagan worship. Wherever blood is shed, there is an altar.

Along with the Scriptures we've looked at about altars, I encourage you to study the covenants God has established with humankind. Several books are available on this topic. One I recommend is *The Covenants* by Kevin Conner and Ken Malmin (City Bible Publishing, 1997). The *Dictionary of Biblical Imagery* talks about the New Covenant and the sacrifice that initiated it, noting that Jesus identified with the altar and that His one sacrifice can be contrasted with all the repeated sacrifices that came before it on other altars. This dictionary refers us to Hebrews 13:10, "We have an altar from which those who serve in the tabernacle have no right to eat," noting that in this passage culminates the New Testament tendency to merge all the images of sacrifice into one in Jesus. It goes on to conclude, "As altar, priest, and sacrifice, Jesus unites all the images associated with biblical altars. He becomes the memorial of the new covenant, the place of sacrifice, and the place of asylum."[6]

The Altar of Prayer

The altar requires sacrifice, prayer, and worship. Our prayers are as sweet incense before God, who is a consuming fire (see Hebrews 12:29). Consistent, passionate prayer is a key to sustaining encounters. Failure to build the altar of prayer will result in a lack of encounters with the Living God. This is when your faith becomes unstable and you can become "a double-minded man, unstable and restless in all his ways [in everything he thinks, feels, or decides]" (James 1:8 AMP).

The lack of encounters creates inconsistencies in your walk of faith. The character and nature of Christ should be reflected through the life of a believer. When you neglect the altar, doubt and unbelief become your constant companions. You then lack assurance that God cares about every detail of your life. You may even lack faith to believe that God hears and answers your prayers. This creates instability since you do not have a conviction of God's intentions and purpose for you.

Consider relationships from a natural perspective. Strong relationships are the direct result of constant interaction and fellowship. It is the same in our relationship with God. When we encounter Him through powerful times of prayer, our conviction is strengthened and our faith increases. This is directly connected with building the altar of prayer.

Several modern-day terms describe this prayer altar. These terms include (but are not limited to) *prayer closet* and *war room*, etc. When we use these terms, we are simply describing intentional times that we set aside for interaction with the Living God. This interaction is not simply our giving Him a list of needs and requests. The altar is the place where we offer the sacrifice of praise and thanksgiving.

Effective, powerful prayer requires that we hear the voice of God and experience His presence, which is encountering Him. "The heartfelt and persistent prayer of a righteous man (believer) can accomplish much [when put into action and made effective by God—it is dynamic and can have tremendous power]" (James 5:16 AMP). When we engage in intense, heartfelt prayer, we are positioned for powerful encounters with the Living God as we cultivate a life marked by His presence. Our times of prayer and interaction with God must exceed familiar patterns of praying religious prayers. We must shift into the realm of dynamic, intense, heartfelt prayers. This type of praying precedes supernatural encounters with the Living God.

> When we engage in intense, heartfelt prayer, we are positioned for powerful encounters with the Living God as we cultivate a life marked by His presence.

Through the power of the Holy Spirit, you have access to God. When we engage in dynamic, intense prayer, we touch God's throne. Another way to understand this is that when we enter the throne room, we access His presence. The result is always a powerful response from heaven. Daniel provides a great example of prayer engagement that leads to powerful encounters:

In those days I, Daniel, had been mourning for three entire weeks. I ate no tasty food, nor did any meat or wine enter my mouth; and I did not anoint (refresh, groom) myself at all for the full three weeks. On the twenty-fourth day of the first month, as I was on the bank of the great river Hiddekel [which is the Tigris], I raised my eyes and looked, and behold, there was a certain man dressed in linen, whose loins were girded with [a belt of] pure gold of Uphaz. His body also was like beryl [with a golden luster], his face had the appearance of lightning, his eyes were like flaming torches, his arms and his feet like the gleam of burnished bronze, and the sound of his words was like the noise of a multitude [of people or the roaring of the sea]. And I, Daniel, alone saw the vision [of this heavenly being], for the men who were with me did not see the vision; nevertheless, a great panic overwhelmed them, so they ran away to hide themselves. So I was left alone and saw this great vision; yet no strength was left in me, for my normal appearance turned to a deathly pale, and I grew weak and faint [with fright]. Then I heard the sound of his words; and when I heard the sound of his words, I fell on my face in a deep sleep, with my face toward the ground.

Daniel 10:2–9 AMP

Consistency in prayer is a key to God-encounters. Daniel understood how to engage in consistent, fervent prayer. Underdevelopment in prayer can prevent you from consistently encountering the Lord. If you accept the truth that God wants to encounter us, and that He has already determined moments in time for encounters to occur in your life, you will begin looking forward to these moments.

When you don't experience consistent encounters with the Lord, it can adversely affect your spiritual walk, and you can also lose the desire for prayer. Here are a few results that can occur when there is a deficiency of God-encounters in your life.

1. *A lack of encounters results in instability in our fellowship with God.* We can find ourselves struggling to set aside consistent times with the Lord, which can create spiritual deficiencies. These spiritual deficiencies result in mediocrity in prayer. We spend more time watching the time than engaging in powerful prayer. While I understand that there are many types of prayer, prayer without passion does not release power. There is no substitute for vibrant, powerful prayer.

2. *Our spiritual life can lack passion and fervor.* Encounters produce conviction. When we encounter the Lord in prayer, our conviction increases, which increases our faith and passion. A way to remain spiritually passionate is through regular encounters.

3. *We miss out on the instruction the Lord can provide during encounters.* During encounters, the Lord can instruct us. These are times when the Lord can give us instructions about our lives, ministry, etc. During encounters, we can hear the Lord's voice with clarity. We are in a position to hear what the Spirit of God is saying to the Church. This is called revelation. We were created to hear the voice of God, and the lack of prayer results in our not accurately hearing God when He speaks.

4. *Our lives become stagnant spiritually and in other ways, which also produces frustration and discouragement.* We overcome stagnation through God-encounters. As we encounter the Lord, our lives are

transformed. Not only that, but we also experience a continual flow of grace and anointing. These blessings are released during times of encounter. Stagnation leads to discouragement and frustration, but encounters result in joy and Kingdom productivity.

I believe one of the reasons many believers don't engage in consistent prayer is because they have not experienced the powerful presence of God that comes through intense praying. Thank God that He has provided all that we need to engage in the supernatural realm, to touch His presence in amazing ways. You and I have access to the Living God. This access helps us become stable in our walk with Him. Too often, we settle for spiritual mediocrity due to an incorrect perception that deeper spiritual matters are for others. The reality is that the Bible, God's manifesto, repeatedly describes His desire for relationship with us. The other reality is that we were designed for and yearn for close contact with Him. These moments of contact are called encounters.

His Name and the Altar

In his book *The Temple of Solomon*, pastor and teacher Kevin Conner writes this about God's name:

The Divine purpose for the existence of the temple is very specific. God wanted to have a place in which to record His Name, a place in which He could dwell among His people in His glory and presence. "The Name" in Scripture always speaks of "the nature" of God, the character of God, who He is and His own essential Being. God has always wanted a place—indeed a PERSON—in which He could set His Name and all that is represented in that expression.[7]

126

God's character and nature are revealed in His names. Each name represents a particular aspect of His nature, and encounters provide opportunities for you to learn of God's nature and ways. God wants a place where He can establish His name. The Tabernacle of Moses, the Tabernacle of David, and Solomon's Temple were physical structures where the name of God was recorded. Now, God's name is recorded in a person. As a believer, God wants His name recorded in you. Conner says of this,

> The ultimate revelation is that God sets His name no longer in a PLACE, but in a PERSON, even the Lord Jesus Christ. And from Him His name is placed upon His people. It is of him 'the whole family in heaven and earth is named' (Ephesians 3:14–15).[8]

The Church is God's temple in which the name of the Lord dwells—forever! We are carriers of the names of God. As we gain revelation of His names, the corresponding aspects of His character are revealed to us. When this happens, conviction, faith, and stability are developed in us.

I want to share this prophecy with you that I heard from the Spirit about God's names: *I am revealing My names to those who will pursue Me. Those who will contend to know Me in a deeper way will encounter Me, as Moses encountered the burning bush. Ask Me for grace to contend for My name, and I will reveal My names to you. I say to you that for as many of My names as you learn and encounter,*

> **We are carriers of the names of God. As we gain revelation of His names, the corresponding aspects of His character are revealed to us.**

*there are yet more to be revealed because I am God, whose
names are an inexhaustible number.*

Pierce and Beeftu say about our relationship with God
and His fire,

> The altar is a place of relationship between God and us—a
> place of pure and wholehearted relationship where our holy
> God can meet with us, and his fire can fall. . . . God created
> us for relationship with him and those around us. The altar
> was established so people could be restored to fellowship
> with him.[9]

Fire is mentioned 508 times in the Modern English Version
of the Bible. This means that it is an important concept to
understand. God's desire is that our hearts would be fully
submitted to Him. When our hearts are fully submitted to
Him, He becomes our priority. When the Lord is our priority, we encounter Him. Encounters keep us focused on the
mandate of heaven. The things that are a priority of heaven
become our priority.

Fire on the Altar

I have had the opportunity to hear more than a few sermon
presentations on the topic of the prophet Elijah and King
Ahab on Mount Carmel. It is probable that you have, too.
Let's look at the story:

> At the time of the offering of the evening sacrifice, Elijah the
> prophet came near and said, "The LORD, God of Abraham,
> Isaac, and of Israel, let it be known this day that You are God
> in Israel and that I am Your servant and that I have done all
> these things at Your word. Hear me, O LORD, hear me, so

that this people may know that You are the LORD God and
that You have turned their hearts back again."

Then the fire of the LORD fell and consumed the burnt
sacrifice and the wood and the stones and the dust and licked
up the water that was in the trench.

When all the people saw it, they fell on their faces and
said, "The LORD, He is God! The LORD, He is God!"

1 Kings 18:36–39

I want to categorize this moment in time as an encounter
between the Kingdom of God and the kingdom of darkness.
Let's begin by looking at three definitions of fire. First and
primarily, fire represents the presence of God, as when Moses
encountered God at the burning bush, and later, when God
appeared in a pillar of fire to lead His people in the wilderness (see Exodus 3:2; 13:21). In Acts 2, the tongues of fire
represent the presence of God the Holy Spirit.

Second, fire refers to the emotions of God. In *The Prophet's Dictionary*, international teacher and minister Paula
Price provides this insight:

Fire . . . is a regularly employed symbolism that depicts the
emotions of God, His use of His elements, and exemplifies
the effects of the Lord's transmission of his word to the
messenger assigned to deliver it. Fire, of all the elements, is
the one that humans can create. This uniqueness makes it
that much more instrumental to prophetic language as the
heat of God's word. Compared to fire, the prophet Jeremiah
said God's word was shut up, burning in his bones. Jeremiah
said that receiving God's prophecies was a fiery experience
to him. Prophetic imagery, too, uses fire in its apparitions
as messenger after messenger are summoned, empowered,
and guided by God's fiery presence. Prophets of today
also find it difficult to comprehend the Lord's words apart

from an appreciation of His elements, particularly that of fire.[10]

Third, fire can refer to God's judgment in Scripture. The context of the story about Elijah and Ahab is based on judgment that had come upon the nation of Israel due to the sin of idolatry. The Bible informs us that King Ahab and Queen Jezebel were wicked rulers. Rather than leading their nation into righteousness, the nation was plunged into idolatry, murder, and varied types of unrighteousness:

> Ahab the son of Omri did more evil in the sight of the LORD than all who were before him. The sins of Jeroboam the son of Nebat were seen as minor for him to walk in, for he took Jezebel the daughter of Ethbaal, king of the Sidonians, as his wife and went and served Baal and worshipped him. He raised an altar for Baal in the house of Baal, which he had built in Samaria. Ahab made an Asherah and did more to provoke the LORD God of Israel to anger than all the kings of Israel who preceded him.
>
> 1 Kings 16:30–33

God's response to the idolatry of the nation was to send judgment. Fire in certain contexts is a representation of God's judgment. The prophet Elijah was sent to declare the word of the Lord: "Now Elijah the Tishbite, who was one of the inhabitants of Gilead, said to Ahab, 'As the LORD God of Israel lives before whom I stand, there will not be dew or rain these years except by my word'" (1 Kings 17:1).

I have noticed the boldness in which Elijah spoke: "There will not be dew or rain these years except by my word." Elijah released the word of the Lord and closed the heavens. Prophets must live in the realm of God-encounters not only to speak forth accurate prophecies, but also that fire might be upon their words. God anoints the mouth and words of prophets and prophetic people who have been in the realm of encounters with Him. He tells His prophets what He is going to do and sends them to declare His word to a people in a particular place at a particular time, and then He performs His word.

Here is a prophetic word I heard from the Holy Spirt about this: *I am indeed revealing prophets whose words will be hot like fire. These firebrand prophets will not eat at Jezebel's table. They will not sell their words or their mouths to the highest bidder. They will not compromise. For some prophets were overtaken by Mammon and Religion in the past seasons. Some will be overtaken in this season. But know this: I have a remnant, who are numbered among My Ekklesia, who will not bow to Jezebel nor eat at her table. They will not be overtaken. They prophesy from the realm of encounters, and My righteousness will be their banner. They carry My fire words for nations and for rulers. They will not back down; neither will they quit. I have trained them in the School of the Spirit, and now I am releasing them!*

Elijah decreed that it would not rain, and it was so. In the course of these pages, I have stated several times that God-encounters result in conviction, and conviction increases our faith. When Elijah boldly declared the season of famine throughout Israel, he had conviction because he had been in the realm of encounters with the Lord. This is what you and I need in order to walk in dominion. The more we occupy the realm of God-encounters, the greater our convictions and our faith. As our faith increases, so does our productivity and accuracy in our Kingdom mandate. It is time for the Church to manifest the works of Jesus. However, we cannot do this without regular encounters with the Lord. I caution you against seeking miracles, signs, and wonders alone. I encourage you to seek the presence of Almighty God, and from that place you will experience visible manifestations of His mighty power working through you.

Throughout the time of famine, Elijah experienced the power of God's provision manifesting in his life. Famine was all around him, yet he was sustained miraculously (see 1 Kings 17:1–6). This is what happens when we learn to live in the realm of encounters. There may be shortages all around you, members of your family may be unemployed, businesses might fail, but God will sustain you in the same way He sustained Elijah. These are some of the results of living in the realm of encounters.

We experience the mighty hand of God working on our behalf not because we sought for things, but because we sought for Him! Even those who come in contact with us and become a conduit of blessings to us experience blessings from God in return (see 1 Kings 17:7–24). Encounters are not just for you. They are for you, the people you are sent to, and those who are assigned to you.

> Encounters are not just for you. They are for you, the people you are sent to, and those who are assigned to you.

Let me give you a principle to help convey this truth. I call it "the principle of priorities": *Prioritize God continually as first in importance in your time and attention, and what you need will find you.* We are commanded to seek first the Kingdom of God and His righteousness, and what we need will be added to us. This is how manifestation comes.

Back at the scene on Mount Carmel, King Ahab, Elijah, and the prophets of Baal assembled for a showdown (see

1 Kings 18:17–40). Elijah declared to the prophets of Baal, "The God that answers by fire, let Him be God" (verse 24). The nation was watching. This was a face-off between the Kingdom of God and the kingdom of darkness. The prophets of Baal built their altar, cut and placed their sacrifice on it, and began to call on Baal from morning to noon. Nothing happened. At noon, they began cutting themselves and prophesying with their blood running, but their god had no voice. There was no response from Baal.

Around 3:00 p.m., which was the hour of prayer, it was Elijah's turn. He prepared the altar of the Lord and put in place twelve stones representing the twelve tribes of Israel. Twelve barrels of water were poured in the trench where the sacrifice lay. Then Elijah prayed,

> The LORD, God of Abraham, Isaac, and of Israel, let it be known this day that You are God in Israel and that I am Your servant and that I have done all these things at Your word. Hear me, O LORD, hear me, so that this people may know that You are the LORD God and that You have turned their hearts back again.
>
> 1 Kings 18:36–37

God responded by consuming the sacrifice, the water, and even the stones. Just as He had done in Egypt against Pharoah, God had again established Himself as the Most High God.

Wicked Altars

Wicked altars are established through sin and disobedience. These altars invoke the power of the kingdom of darkness. The entertainment industry has pushed forth an effort to deceive people into thinking that witchcraft and divination are acceptable. The *Harry Potter* series has done much harm to children by way of influencing them to believe that magic arts and casting spells are fine and fun. To make this lie acceptable, we often hear things like, "It's all in fun" or "I'm helping people with my ability."

It becomes particularly egregious when we have high-profile sports figures, singers, and actors promoting these dark arts. I recently heard a story on the evening news about a high-profile sports figure who had turned to astrology and was starting to give people readings to help him develop. I wondered how much media coverage he would have been given if his testimony had been that he received Jesus as his Lord and Savior and he was taking opportunities to pray for people. I also saw another story about a man who was wearing a shirt with the inscription *Jesus is the only way to salvation*. He was going into a restaurant and was declined seating because of his shirt. There is a zero tolerance policy in our culture for the Church.

Earlier in this chapter we looked at some Scriptures about evil altars, but here are a few more examples of these wicked places:

> Ahaz was twenty years old when he became king, and he reigned for sixteen years in Jerusalem. He did not do what was right in the sight of the Lord his God like David his father. He walked in the way of the kings of Israel and even made his son pass through the fire according to the abominations of the nations whom the Lord dispossessed before the children of Israel. He sacrificed and made offerings on the high places, on the hills, and under every green tree.
>
> 2 Kings 16:2–4

They caused their sons and daughters to pass through the fire, used divination and omens, and sold themselves to do evil in the sight of the LORD to anger Him.

2 Kings 17:17

But each nation was making its own gods, and they put them in the houses of the high places that the people of Samaria had made, each nation in the cities where they were living. . . . The Avvites made Nibhaz and Tartak. The Sepharvites were burning their children in fire to Adrammelek and Anammelek, the gods of Sepharvaim.

2 Kings 17:29–31

He [Manasseh] built altars for all the host of heaven in the two courts of the house of the LORD. He made his son pass through the fire, was conjuring and seeking omens, and dealt with mediums and soothsayers. He did much evil in the sight of the LORD, provoking Him to anger.

He put a carved image of Asherah that he had made in the house of which the LORD said to David and to Solomon his son, "In this house and in Jerusalem, which I have chosen out of all tribes of Israel, I will put My name forever."

2 Kings 21:5–7

Keep the Fire Burning

Fire is necessary to burn the sacrifice. In Solomon's dedication of the Temple, the number of sheep and oxen offered could not be counted. That's a picture of sacrifice!

King Solomon and all the congregation of Israel who were assembled before him stood together in front of the ark, sacrificing so many sheep and oxen that they could not be told or numbered. . . .

135

> And when the priests came out of the holy place, the cloud filled the house of the Lord, so that the priests could not continue to minister because of the cloud, for the glory of the Lord filled the house of the Lord.
>
> 1 Kings 8:5, 10–11

The greatest picture of all depicting sacrifice, however, can be seen in Jesus, the Lamb who was slain. "Worthy is the Lamb who was slain, to receive power and riches and wisdom and strength and honor and glory and blessing!" (Revelation 5:12). Jesus paid the ultimate price to redeem us, thereby providing us with access to the Father. We are to present our bodies as a living sacrifice before God. This means we are the sacrifice on the altar. Those who desire to follow God must be willing to forsake everything (see Matthew 6:33; Mark 8:34). This does not mean that we are to leave our families and quit our jobs. It means that God must take first priority in our lives.

Life is filled with distractions. Some are subtle, others more visible. If you develop what I call "the principle of first"— *seek God first*—you can manage the distractions that come. A key to keeping the fire burning and sustaining God's presence is knowing that whatever you sacrifice for the Kingdom of God brings a blessing to your life. You may be wondering how you can tell what God wants you to sacrifice. We can know the will of God. Don't get into unbalanced, spooky living. Jesus was not weird and unbalanced. He listened for the voice of His Father and followed His directions. Jesus did what He saw His Father do (see John 5:19). He is our example.

To keep the fire burning, contend against distractions, discouragement, and disruptions. The enemy will send opposition against you to overwhelm you. If you focus more on what is happening around you than on what God wants to do through you and for you, you will be overwhelmed.

Maintaining your focus will come as you prioritize your relationship with God above all else.

Contending creates a conviction within you to keep your altar strong and active as you overcome distractions and spiritual disturbances. The reality is that the kingdom of darkness wants you to lose courage and give up. The apostle Paul understood the importance of creating the spiritual capacity to contend:

> I do not count myself to have attained, but this one thing I do, forgetting those things which are behind and reaching forward to those things which are ahead, I press toward the goal to the prize of the high calling of God in Christ Jesus.
>
> Therefore let those of us who are mature be thus minded. And if you think differently in any way, God will reveal even this to you.
>
> Philippians 3:13–15

Contending occurs in every 24-hour cycle of time. It is part of our cycle of sacrifice. We die daily to the agenda of self and come alive to the agenda of the Most High God (see 1 Corinthians 15:31).

Cultivating the practice of constant worship also keeps the fire burning. God is looking for those who will worship Him in Spirit and in truth (see John 4:24). Worship is a key activity of heaven that happens constantly. When you create an atmosphere of worship, you have created the atmosphere of heaven. This is where encounters occur. You are a spiritual being living in an earthen vessel. Yet you carry the immeasurable glory of God in your body, your earthen vessel:

> But we have this treasure in earthen vessels, the excellency of the power being from God and not from ourselves. We are

troubled on every side, yet not distressed; we are perplexed, but not in despair; persecuted, but not forsaken; cast down, but not destroyed; and always carrying around in the body the death of the Lord Jesus, that also the life of Jesus might be expressed in our bodies. For we who live are always delivered to death for Jesus' sake, that also the life of Jesus might be manifested in our mortal flesh.

2 Corinthians 4:7–11

Worship enlarges you, creating the capacity to see God move in and around you. Worship fans the flames and sets you ablaze!

Don't settle for spiritual mediocrity. Too many believers are not walking in their inheritance as sons and daughters of the Kingdom. Rather than walking as kings and priests in the earth, too many believers settle for whatever happens in their lives. An encounter shifts the status quo in your life. Your conviction increases as the result of an encounter. An encounter with the healing presence of God creates conviction and enlarges your faith to believe that if He healed you of migraine headaches, He can also heal you of arthritis. This is how conviction works. Our resolve is strengthened. Faith comes alive, and manifestation occurs (see Romans 8:17; Hebrews 6:17; James 2:5). When you seek God with all your heart, mediocrity is broken because He responds and brings you into new dimensions of your walk with Him. "Then you shall call upon Me, and you shall come and pray to Me, and I will listen to you. You shall seek Me and find Me, when you shall search for Me with all your heart" (Jeremiah 29:12–13).

Keep the fire burning by keeping your shield of faith active. "And above all, taking the shield of faith, with which you will be able to extinguish all the fiery arrows of the evil one"

(Ephesians 6:16). Faith is the key that unlocks the promises of God. "And without faith it is impossible to please God, for he who comes to God must believe that He exists and that He is a rewarder of those who diligently seek Him" (Hebrews 11:6).

The Bible is God's written manifesto containing His will for you. It tells you why God created you. Like King David, we must hide God's Word in our hearts. Faith is not belief-ism. Faith is trusting in what God has said He will do. "Now faith is the substance of things hoped for, the evidence of things not seen" (Hebrews 11:1).

In every season we must repair our altar, which means we are positioning ourselves to receive God's fire. Each day, you and I must be willing to get on the altar and allow the fire of God to fall upon our lives (see Exodus 3:2; Psalm 5:3 MESSAGE; Psalm 104:4; 1 Corinthians 13:3; Hebrews 12:29). These things we have just looked at are some of the ways you can keep fire on the altar—keeping the fire of God burning within you.

PRAYER ACTIVATION

Lord, give me grace to daily contend for the "principle of priorities." Help me keep You first. I decree that I will build the altar of prayer and presence. I will bring to You the sacrifice of praise and thanksgiving. The fruit of my lips will give You praise. I decree that every morning, I will lay out the pieces of my life on the altar before You and wait for fresh fire to fall on me. Baptize me with fire, that I might encounter You in the midst of the flames, in Jesus' name.

EIGHT

Sustaining Encounters

After this I looked. And there was an open door in heaven. The first voice I heard was like a trumpet speaking with me, saying, "Come up here, and I will show you things which must take place after this." Immediately I was in the Spirit. And there was a throne set in heaven with One sitting on the throne!

Revelation 4:1–2

If you lack understanding of the principles that govern God-encounters, you are at risk of violating them, and in so doing, hindering the flow of encounters in your life. You will not be able to sustain a life of encounters if you are violating the patterns and principles that govern this realm. If you follow these patterns and principles, however, you will increasingly encounter God in amazing ways.

I want to discuss a few of these principles in more detail. The eight principles we will look at here include (1) *resist pride*, (2) *know what and when to share*, (3) *avoid spooky* behavior, (4) *pursue the interpretation of an encounter*, (5) *prepare in prayer*, (6) *walk in purity*, (7) *develop patience*, and (8) *live a life of obedience*. These eight principles are not the only ones that govern encounters, but they are each important for us to understand and follow.

Principle 1: Resist pride.

Encounters are for our growth and development, not our entertainment. These are not moments in time that occur to fill our spiritual résumé with boasting rights. When you begin to enter into the realm of encounters, it is important to walk in humility before the Lord. "God resists the proud, but gives grace to the humble" (James 4:6). Connect to mature believers who are sound in the Word of God and who can help you understand your encounter experiences. (See Leviticus 26:19; 2 Chronicles 26:16; Job 41; Psalm 10:4; Proverbs 16:18; 1 Peter 5:5.)

Principle 2: Know when and what to share.

There will be times of encounter that are shareable. There will also be times when, like the apostle Paul, you will be limited by the Holy Spirit and be prevented from sharing. Not all God-encounter events are shareable. You might have the most amazing encounter, and then the Holy Spirit will instruct you not to share it. This is for your protection and can prevent you from entering into pride. This is why you must develop sensitivity to the Spirit of God.

There is a sacredness that marks encounters. Some encounters may have restrictions that accompany them, like being forbidden to discuss them, or some aspect of them, with others. The apostle Paul was not allowed to repeat some of the things he heard during one encounter. He describes a man [presumably himself] being "caught up in an ecstatic experience and brought into paradise, where he overheard many wonderous and inexpressible secrets that were so sacred that no mortal is permitted to repeat them" (2 Corinthians 12:4 TPT).

> You must develop the practice of asking the Lord whether or not an encounter experience should be shared, and with whom.

In the book of Revelation, John had a similar experience: "And when the seven thunders sounded their voices, I was about to write, but I heard a voice from heaven saying to me, 'Seal up those things which the seven thunders said, and do not write them'" (Revelation 10:4). You must develop the practice of asking the Lord whether or not an encounter experience should be shared, and with whom.

Principle 3: Avoid spooky behavior.

I encourage you to avoid spooky behavior. Several years ago, believers began experiencing encounters of laughter. These sacred moments restored joy to many believers, some of whom were emotionally depressed. These were amazing joy encounters. Some believers, however, would leave corporate gatherings while they were yet under the power of the Holy Spirit. They would go into restaurants while still displaying loud, boisterous laughter. Some even fell down in public places. This is an example of spooky behavior. Unbelievers didn't understand this behavior and simply dismissed believers as being weird or spooky.

What I am saying is that not every encounter is for the world at large. God will bring you into sacred places to express some truths that He wants you to know for your own benefit and admonition. Sometimes it will be a secret that God wants to share just with you in that moment. There will also be other times, however, when you will experience encounters that you can share with others in an effort to build their faith to believe that God wants them to have encounters, too.

We have already seen how in Scripture, the apostle Paul provides us with the details of a powerful encounter he experienced. Yet he remained balanced. He didn't become weird or spooky. He used his experience as a teaching opportunity for believers, telling us in 2 Corinthians 12:1–4 (TPT),

> Although it may not accomplish a thing, I need to move on and boast about supernatural visions and revelations of the Lord. Someone I'm acquainted with, who is in union with Christ, was swept away fourteen years ago in an ecstatic experience. He was taken into the third heaven, but I'm not sure if he was in his body or out of his body—only God knows. And I know that this man (again, I'm not sure if he was still in his body or taken out of his body—God knows) was caught up in an ecstatic experience and brought into paradise, where he overheard many wondrous and inexpressible secrets that were so sacred that no mortal is permitted to repeat them.

Principle 4: Pursue the interpretation of an encounter.

Like prophecy, encounters must be interpreted through Scripture. Encounters are designed to bring us into places of greater conviction, and then into enlargement of our faith. Another way to understand conviction is to understand assurance. Conviction gives us the assurance of truth. From a legal perspective, to convict someone means to deliver a verdict of guilty. This suggests finality in the decision. From a spiritual perspective, believers can waver in their under-standing of God and His purpose for them. This leads to double-mindedness, discouragement, frustration, and some-times resentment against God. Spending time in the study of God's Word, the Bible, will help you access the revelation to interpret your encounter.

Principle 5: Prepare in prayer.

In the absence of prayer fellowship with the Lord, we become susceptible to deception. As our faith increases, we can then begin greater Kingdom productivity and advance-ment. Growing in prayer also creates stability and reality in our walk with Christ. While this is true for all believ-ers, I have noticed a deficiency of supernatural encounters among our youth. The emergence of violent video games and other malevolent behaviors makes it critical for the Millennial and Z generations to align with spiritual fathers and mothers in the faith, who can disciple them in God's Word and in godly living. This will prepare them for su-pernatural encounters.

In a culture where there is tolerance for every name ex-cept the name of Jesus, effective Kingdom discipleship pro-grams are key for the times we live in. There is an increase in witchcraft, humanism, and sexual immorality, and we can see issues stemming from the manifesto of darkness on social media and entertainment platforms. These is-sues necessitate the urgency of younger generations being immersed in the culture of the Kingdom of God. This can be accomplished through the practice of consistent prayer. The good news is that they want to be discipled. These gen-erations want authentic encounters with the Living Jesus, not dead religion.

Principle 6: Walk in purity.

Our motives must always remain pure. Daily allow the Lord to purify your heart. Remember that encounters are one of the ways God brings you close to Him. In these moments, you experience His restoring presence.

King David understood the need for experiencing the restorative presence of God. He wrote in Psalm 23:3, "He restores my soul; He leads me in paths of righteousness for His name's sake." (See also Psalm 24:4; 51:7, 10; Malachi 3:3; Hebrews 10:22; James 4:8.)

Principle 7: Develop patience.

You must have the capacity for being patient. Be willing to wait. "But those who wait upon the LORD shall renew their strength; they shall mount up with wings as eagles, they shall run and not be weary, and they shall walk and not faint" (Isaiah 40:31). Patience is developed over time. God uses the circumstances around you to create the necessary capacity for patience within you (see Romans 8:26–28). He doesn't waste anything. He works all things out for your good, but you must cultivate patience. A harvest of encounters will come, if you will learn to wait. (See Romans 5; Galatians 5:22; Ephesians 4:2; Colossians 1:11; 2 Thessalonians 1:4; 1 Timothy 6:11.)

Principle 8: Live a life of obedience.

God requires obedience. Our submission to Him is an indication that we trust Him to bring us into every promise He has made to us. As we live a life of obedience, we can trust that whatever our circumstances, God watches over His Word to perform it:

For as the rain comes down, and the snow from heaven, and do not return there but water the earth and make it bring forth and bud that it may give seed to the sower and bread to the eater, so shall My word be that goes forth from My mouth; it shall not return to Me void, but it shall accomplish that which I please, and it shall prosper in the thing for which I sent it.

Isaiah 55:10–11

We can also trust that living a life of obedience will bring us into the realm of God-encounters that will strengthen and transform us in our relationship with Him. (See Deuteronomy 28:10; Psalm 81:10–12; Romans 10:3; James 4:7; 1 Peter 1:22.)

Types of Encounters

We have discussed several types of encounters throughout this book. We primarily hear about the type of encounters we consider more "spectacular," like Ezekiel being caught up by a lock of his hair, suspended between heaven and earth, and shown amazing things (see Ezekiel 8). Or what about Isaiah's amazing vision of the Lord, whose train was filling the Temple (see Isaiah 6)? These are just two examples of encounters that can be considered more spectacular. If you only focus on this type of encounter, however, you might miss a supernatural encounter that is more subtle. The more subtle types could be a healing encounter or an encounter in the Word of God. Any supernatural encounter initiated by God has great significance and should not be overlooked.

Encounters must be interpreted so that you gain the revelation God is sending to you. We advance God's Kingdom mandate through revelation. When you encounter heaven, you are being transformed. As I have said throughout these pages, encounters bring conviction, which strengthens your faith. When your faith is strengthened, you gain stability in your faith life. A stable faith life creates the necessary spiritual paradigm to advance God's Kingdom mandate effectively. Encounters are an inherent component of God's manifesto. Therefore, it is vital to understand encounters from God's perspective. When you are grounded in a biblical understanding of supernatural encounters that are initiated by God,

> **Any supernatural encounter initiated by God has great significance and should not be overlooked.**

you will also be able to recognize those moments that are initiated by the kingdom of darkness. Remember, encounters must be interpreted, and any encounter that does not agree with Scripture must be rejected.

To help you gain an even greater understanding of God-encounters, in the rest of this chapter we will look a little more closely at the various types of encounters you may experience. These include (but are not limited to) vision encounters, dream encounters, angelic encounters, Word encounters, commissioning encounters, prayer encounters, healing encounters, and deliverance and protection encounters. I will also provide some Scripture references to assist you in your journey of gaining understanding of these various ways in which you may encounter God.

Vision encounters

A God-encounter can occur as a vision. Visions can occur while you are awake. Paula Price defines them in *The Prophet's Dictionary* as "Seeing the events or manifestation of the supernatural world with awakened and elevated natural

faculties. (Genesis 15:1; Isaiah 1:1; Daniel 9:23)."[1] Peter and
Cornelius experienced a vision encounter of an angel revealing God's intent of salvation for the Gentiles (see Acts 10).
Three of the disciples experienced a vision encounter on top
of a mountain with Jesus:

> After six days Jesus took Peter, James, and John his brother
> and brought them up to a high mountain alone, and was
> transfigured before them. His face shone as the sun, and His
> garments became white as the light. Suddenly Moses and
> Elijah appeared to them, talking with Him.
>
> Matthew 17:1–3

Dream encounters

When prophetically spurred, dreams send messages and
information conveyed by the Lord, or by His spiritual agen-
cies such as an angel. These encounters take the form of a
prophetic dream. While people are asleep, God shows them
something that pertains to or affects their waking sphere of
life. This differs in context from a vision. Dream encounters
aim to open a dreamer's natural faculties to receive the vision, apart from the person's natural understanding. Dream
encounters give revelatory information that the person would
not otherwise know. Look at the dream encounters of Jacob
and Solomon:

> Then Jacob went out from Beersheba and went toward
> Harran. He came to a certain place and stayed there all night
> because the sun had set. He took one of the stones of that
> place and put it under his head, and lay down in that place
> to sleep. *He dreamed and saw a ladder set up on the earth
> with the top of it reaching to heaven. The angels of God
> were ascending and descending on it. The Lord stood above*

148

it and said, "I am the LORD God of Abraham your father and the God of Isaac. The land on which you lie, to you will I give it and to your descendants."

Genesis 28:10–13, emphasis added

While he was in Gibeon, *the Lord appeared to Solomon in a dream at night*, and He said, "Ask what you want from Me."

Solomon answered, "You have shown great mercy to your servant David my father, because he walked before You in faithfulness, righteousness, and uprightness of heart toward You. And You have shown him great kindness in giving him a son to sit on his throne this day.

"Now, O LORD, my God, You have made Your servant king in place of my father David, and I am still a little child and do not know how to go out or come in. And Your servant is in the midst of Your people whom You have chosen, a great people, so numerous that they cannot be numbered or counted. Give Your servant therefore an understanding heart to judge Your people, that I may discern between good and bad, for who is able to judge among so great a people?"

It pleased the Lord that Solomon had asked this. God said to him, "Because you have asked this and have not asked for yourself long life or riches or the lives of your enemies, but have asked for yourself wisdom so that you may have discernment in judging, I now do according to your words. I have given you a wise and an understanding heart, so that there has never been anyone like you in the past, and there shall never arise another like you. I have also given you what you have not asked, both riches and honor, so that no kings will compare to you all of your days. If you will walk in My ways, keeping My statutes and My commandments as your father David did, then I will lengthen your days." *Solomon awoke and found it was a dream.*

1 Kings 3:5–15, emphasis added

Angelic encounters

God uses divine messengers to execute His purposes. In her book *Angels in God's Kingdom*, Dr. Barbie Breathitt writes,

> They are heavenly beings with great beauty and intelligence. God dispatches these messengers to carry out the government of Heaven on Earth. Angels who offer their loyal allegiance to serve God, are called "the angels of God" (John 1:51). Angels are called "evil" or "unclean spirits," if they are of the one-third of the angels who fell with Lucifer (Luke 8:2; 11:24, 26).[2]

Angelic encounters happen throughout the Bible. An angel appeared to Joseph and instructed him to take his family and escape into Egypt (see Matthew 2:13). Peter also experienced an angelic encounter. Having been arrested by King Herod, Peter was sleeping, bound by chains, between two soldiers. He was awakened by an angel and led out of prison (see Acts 12). Look at the angelic encounters of Elijah and Zechariah:

> As he [Elijah] lay and slept under the juniper tree, *an angel touched him and said to him,* "Arise and eat." He looked, and there was a cake baked on coals and a jar of water at his head. And he ate and drank and then lay down again.
>
> *The angel of the* Lord *came again a second time* and touched him and said, "Arise and eat, because the journey is too great for you." He arose and ate and drank and went in the strength of that food forty days and forty nights to Horeb, the mountain of God.
>
> 1 Kings 19:5–8, emphasis added

> *Then an angel of the Lord appeared to him,* standing on the right side of the altar of incense. When Zechariah saw him,

he was troubled, and fear fell upon him. But the angel said to him, "Do not fear, Zechariah, for your prayer has been heard, and your wife Elizabeth will bear you a son, and you shall call his name John. You will have joy and gladness, and many will rejoice at his birth."

Luke 1:11–14, emphasis added

Word encounters

It is not uncommon for the word of the Lord and visions to be part of a singular encounter. We both hear something and see something in these moments. Look at the word encounters Abram and Ezekiel experienced:

After this *the word of the* LORD *came to Abram in a vision*, saying,

"Do not fear, Abram. I am your shield, your exceedingly great reward."

But Abram said, "Lord GOD, what will You give me, seeing I am childless and the heir of my house is Eliezer of Damascus?" Abram said, "Since You have not given me any children, my heir is a servant born in my house."

Then the word of the LORD came to him, saying, "This man will not be your heir, but a son that is from your own body will be your heir." He brought him outside and said, "Look up toward heaven and count the stars, if you are able to count them." And He said to him, "So will your descendants be."

Genesis 15:1–5, emphasis added

As I was among the captives by the river of Kebar, the heavens were opened and *I saw visions of God*.

On the fifth day of the month, which was the fifth year of the captivity of King Jehoiachin, *the word of the* LORD *came expressly to Ezekiel* the priest, the son of Buzi, in the land of the Chaldeans by the River Kebar. And the hand of the LORD was on him there.

As I looked, a whirlwind came out of the north, a great cloud with fire flashing forth continually, and a brightness was all around it, and in its midst something as glowing metal in the midst of the fire.

Ezekiel 1:1–4, emphasis added

Commissioning encounters

There are also God-encounters where the Lord commissions the receiver to carry out a task to accomplish heaven's agenda. Here are Jeremiah's commissioning encounter, and Joshua's commissioning to take Israel into the Promised Land:

But the LORD said to me, "Do not say, 'I am a youth.' *For you shall go everywhere that I send you, and whatever I command you, you shall speak.* Do not be afraid of their faces. For I am with you to deliver you," says the LORD.

Then the LORD put forth His hand and touched my mouth. And the LORD said to me, "Now, I have put My words in your mouth. See, I have this day set you over the nations and over the kingdoms, to root out and to pull down, to destroy and to throw down, to build and to plant."

Jeremiah 1:7–10, emphasis added

Now after the death of Moses the servant of the LORD, the LORD spoke to Joshua son of Nun, the assistant of Moses: "Moses My servant is dead, so *now get up and cross over the Jordan—you and all this people*—to the land that I am giving to the children of Israel. I have given you every place that the sole of your foot shall tread, as I said to Moses."

Joshua 1:1–3, emphasis added

Prayer encounters

Prayer is a place of encountering God and growing in relationship with Him. It is where we position ourselves for an encounter by stepping into the supernatural realm to commune with God. Though you may not know it in the beginning of the journey, when you look back over some months and years, you start getting insights. You get new perspectives about yourself, about God, and about His Kingdom. Here is an example of a prayer encounter Daniel had:

> *While I was speaking and praying* and confessing my sin and the sin of my people Israel, and presenting my supplication before the LORD my God for the holy mountain of my God, *indeed, while I was speaking in prayer*, the man Gabriel, whom I had seen in the vision at the beginning, being caused to fly swiftly, touched me about the time of the evening oblation. He informed me and talked with me, and said, "Daniel, I have now come to give you insight and understanding. At the beginning of your supplications the command went out, and I have come to tell you, for you are greatly beloved. Therefore understand the matter and consider the vision."
>
> Daniel 9:20–23, emphasis added

Healing encounters

Healing encounters are moments when we experience supernatural healing. The tangible presence and power of God comes upon us, resulting in healing. These encounters are available regardless of how significant the medical condition is. Peter's mother-in-law had such a healing encounter with Jesus:

> He went out of the synagogue and entered Simon's house. Now Simon's mother-in-law was taken ill with a high fever,

and they asked Him about her. So He stood over her and rebuked the fever, and it left her. And immediately she rose and served them.

Luke 4:38–39

A man who had been lame from birth experienced a healing encounter at the Temple gate called Beautiful when Peter commanded him to rise and walk in the name of Jesus (see Acts 3:1–10). Healing encounters are part of our spiritual inheritance made available through the death, burial, and resurrection of Jesus (see Isaiah 53:5; Matthew 4:24; 8:13; Luke 4:40; 5:15; 1 Peter 2:24).

Deliverance and protection encounters

The types of encounters involving deliverance and protection occur in dire circumstances and adverse situations. Often, the person having such an encounter is at risk of harm or death. Supernatural engagement is released on behalf of the individual, protecting and delivering him or her from harm. In the Old Testament, Shadrach, Meshach, and Abednego had such an encounter. In the New Testament, Paul and Silas had this type of encounter in prison.

Then Nebuchadnezzar was full of fury. . . . He commanded the most mighty men in his army to bind Shadrach, Meshach, and Abednego and cast them into the burning fiery furnace. Then these men were bound in their trousers, their coats, and their hats, and their other garments, and were cast into the midst of the burning fiery furnace. Therefore, because the king's commandment was urgent and the furnace exceeding hot, the flame of the fire killed those men who took up Shadrach, Meshach, and Abednego. These three men, Shadrach, Meshach, and Abednego, fell down bound into the midst of the burning fiery furnace.

Then Nebuchadnezzar the king was astonished, and rose up in haste, and spoke, and said to his counselors, "Did we not cast three men bound into the midst of the fire?"

They answered and said to the king, "True, O king."

He answered and said, *"But I see four men loose and walking in the midst of the fire, and they are unharmed. And the form of the fourth is like the Son of God!"*

Daniel 3:19–25, emphasis added

Having received such an order, he [the jailer] threw them into the inner prison and fastened their feet in the stocks.

At midnight Paul and Silas were praying and singing hymns to God, and the prisoners were listening to them. Suddenly there was a great earthquake, so that the foundations of the prison were shaken. And immediately all the doors were opened and everyone's shackles were loosened.

Acts 16:24–26

The Effects of Encounters

Daniel provides us with an account of a God-encounter that had numerous effects on him. First, it caused him to fall facedown and even become mute. Then the encounter also strengthened him:

When he had spoken such words to me, I set my face toward the ground, and I became mute. Then one in the likeness of the sons of men touched my lips. Then I opened my mouth and spoke and said to him who stood before me, "O my lord, because of the vision, sorrows have come upon me, and I have retained no strength. How can the servant of my lord talk with you, my lord? And as for me, there remains no strength in me now, nor is there any breath left in me."

Then again, the one having the appearance of a man came and touched me, and he strengthened me. He said, "O man, greatly beloved, do not fear. Peace be unto you. Be strong and courageous!"

When he spoke to me, I was strengthened and said, "Let my lord speak, for you have strengthened me."

Daniel 10:15–19

In chapter 6, we looked at a passage from the book of Isaiah in which the prophet provided us with an amazingly detailed account of an encounter he had with the Lord. Let's look at the encounter again in another translation and take note of the effects it had on him. It both allowed him to see his own spiritual condition and to receive cleansing:

In the year that King Uzziah died, I saw [in a vision] the Lord sitting on a throne, high and exalted, with the train of His royal robe filling the [most holy part of the] temple. Above Him seraphim (heavenly beings) stood; each one had six wings: with two wings he covered his face, with two wings he covered his feet, and with two wings he flew. And one called out to another, saying,

"Holy, Holy, Holy is the LORD of hosts;
The whole earth is filled with His glory."

And the foundations of the thresholds trembled at the voice of him who called out, and the temple was filling with smoke. Then I said,

"Woe is me! For I am ruined,
Because I am a man of [ceremonially] unclean lips,

And I live among a people of unclean lips;
For my eyes have seen the King, the LORD of hosts."

Then one of the seraphim flew to me with a burning coal in his hand, which he had taken from the altar with tongs. He touched my mouth with it and said, "Listen carefully, this has touched your lips; your wickedness [your sin, your injustice, your wrongdoing] is taken away and your sin atoned for and forgiven."

Isaiah 6:1–7 AMP

Additional Scriptures

We have examined several types of encounters, yet the examples and Scriptures I have presented are by no means exhaustive. Many more examples can be found in the Bible. I encourage you to prayerfully study the Scriptures in this chapter, as well as studying these additional Scriptures: Genesis 20; 28:10–22; Exodus 3:2; Numbers 12:6; Deuteronomy 13:1–3; Judges 6:12; 13:3; Daniel 6:22; Joel 2:28; Matthew 1:18–25; 2:13–15, 19–23; Acts 2:17; Revelation 22:6.

In our next two chapters, we will discuss some frequently asked questions about encounters, and then we will look at some additional testimonies given by individuals who have experienced powerful supernatural encounters. I will conclude after that with some final thoughts at the end, and some actions you can take to live a life of amazing supernatural encounters with the Living God.

PRAYER ACTIVATION

Lord, open my eyes to see and understand Your patterns, processes, and principles. Help me recognize encounters that You have initiated. I am committed to knowing You in a deeper way. Deliver me from any bondage of spiritual laziness that would prevent me from knowing the deep things of Your Spirit. In Jesus' name, Amen.

NINE

FAQs about Encounters

My focus in this book has been to bring clarity and greater understanding to the subject of supernatural encounters. Now that you have read these pages and have seen some of the Scriptures that show us encounters with the Living God, I encourage you to spend time in His presence and continue in the study of His Word. These practices will help you live a life of God-encounters and discern the source of the encounters you experience.

You will also gain understanding of how God speaks to you. Uninterpreted encounters can result in not having a complete understanding of what God is saying. An example of this can be seen in having a revelatory dream. You know God is saying something in the dream; you just aren't sure what. Interpretation brings clarity and conviction.

Understanding God-encounters and their interpretation, however, can be a challenge. Because of that, I queried several believers and invited them to submit their questions on the subject. Perhaps you have the same questions they did. It's possible that my responses to their questions will further clarify your understanding of supernatural encounters. I am therefore including the following "frequently asked questions" about encounters here, along with the answers for you. As you continue learning about this topic, the important thing is to remember that God *wants* you to encounter Him. That is His manifesto—relationship with us!

Are encounters important? Are they for today?

Encounters with God are an important aspect of a believer's life. Encounters increase conviction and enlarge our faith. In addition, they provide the opportunity for us to learn more about God's ways and His nature. These factors help us be more productive in our Kingdom mandate since we are declaring God from a position of experience and not just theology. Anytime you touch the supernatural realm, this is an encounter, whether you are receiving a revelatory message, healing, or deliverance. The source is the supernatural realm. A lack of encounters can result in unbelief and discouragement in your faith walk. God desires to reveal aspects of Himself and His plans to you. Let faith arise in you and ask God to help you not miss these moments.

Would having encounters make God more real to me?

Encounters bring conviction, and conviction activates your faith. The interaction in a supernatural encounter reveals aspects of God's character and nature, which in turn gives us conviction about the reality of whatever God is showing us. Deliverance and healing encounters display God's love and mercy toward us as He takes away disease and replaces it with wholeness. Encounters have a purpose. For example, some years ago there was an emergence of holy laughter.

Believers would become "drunk in the Spirit" and laugh uncontrollably. These were supernatural moments. Consider a believer who has been battling depression, and then suddenly the supernatural realm opens and this person receives supernatural joy, causing him or her to break out of the prison of depression. These God-inspired moments show us the reality of God.

Do encounters make you more spiritual or more special to God than someone else is?

No. Perceiving yourself as more spiritual or special than someone else because of an encounter is the work of pride. When you allow pride to puff you up, you have missed the point of the encounter. Encounters bring us closer to an aspect of God's character and nature. Humility is most often the emotion we experience. As I said earlier, humility is the common thread among people I have known who have amazing testimonies of supernatural encounters with Jesus. Humility helps us maintain balance and avoid going into error. I caution you to walk in humility. As with Isaiah, our human condition pales in light of the glorious majesty of God.

What are some ways you can maintain encounters?

In chapter 7, you will find several principles regarding the altar of sacrifice we must establish in our lives, and the ways we can maintain fire on that altar. Our spiritual development requires that we build and maintain such an altar, because our growth and development require daily commitment. When we are intentional about seeking God, He will respond by encountering us. In chapter 8, you will find a list of principles that govern God-encounters. These principles include (but are not limited to) resisting pride, knowing what and when to share, avoiding spooky behavior, pursuing the interpretation of an encounter, preparing in prayer, walking in purity, developing patience, and living a life of obedience. (You can learn more about all these important principles by reading those chapters.) When you implement these principles on a daily basis, you create an environment for maintaining encounters with God.

I have had encounters, but they don't seem to be big and exciting. Is something wrong?

No. Encounters like Isaiah, Ezekiel, and Jacob had are often the ones we use as the model for encounters. While these models highlight incredible moments, the moments you experience that seemingly aren't as "spectacular" really are astonishing in their own right. Anytime we step into the realm of the supernatural, those are amazing moments. As I said in the previous chapter, any supernatural encounter initiated by God has great significance and should not be overlooked. On one occasion, I had a prayer encounter. I had been studying the Bible and some other materials most of the day. Throughout this time, I was also engaging in prayer. Suddenly, the Lord spoke one word to me—just one single word. Yet that word exploded within me. My room filled with His glory and presence, and I began to weep. It was the word I needed in that moment. One word from God makes a difference. Never discount God-initiated encounters.

Should I seek and pray for specific kinds of encounters, like angelic visitations, or should I ask for encounters and be satisfied with whatever comes?

I don't think there's a problem with asking for specific kinds of encounters, like angelic visitations. As I mentioned earlier, one time I spent weeks praying and asking God to "take me to His throne room." I believe there are certain experiences that God wants us to have, and He will create a desire in us to ask Him for them. I caution you to remember, however, that our priority should be to seek after God Himself. We are to seek first the Kingdom of God and its righteousness. If we seek for God, He will reveal Himself. He has told us, "Call to Me, and I will answer you, and show you great and mighty things which you do not know" (Jeremiah 33:3). We are not told to seek experiences. When we primarily seek after experiences, we are at risk of overlooking God's reason for wanting us to encounter Him. Ask and it shall be given, but don't lose focus on the One who does the giving.

Is fasting necessary to have encounters? How long do I have to fast and pray before I receive an encounter?

I wouldn't set a time restraint concerning how long a fast should be. I would encourage you to be led of the Spirit in fasting. But by all means, fast. Fasting acts as an accelerant to our prayer life. It is a necessary component to building an altar of prayer and worship, and to submission. It kindles the fire on our altar and exposes soulish issues in us that need to be overcome. Fasting should be a necessary part of every believer's life. As believers, we are expected to fast and pray. Jesus expected that we would do both, saying, "When you pray . . . Moreover, when you fast . . ." (Matthew 6:5, 16).

This is how we bring our soul and body under subjection to the Holy Spirit. Moreover, having dominion begins with having dominion over yourself (see 2 Corinthians 10:3–6). Fasting helps you overcome unbelief and renews your faith. Fasting helps sharpen your spiritual senses to perceive God more easily. Jesus had encounters after He fasted (see Matthew 4). In the book of Daniel, we see that that Daniel wasn't praying for an encounter (see Daniel 9). He was fasting and praying because he had received a prophetic message and a vision concerning future events that grieved him:

> In the third year of Cyrus king of Persia a message was re-
> vealed to Daniel, whose name was called Belteshazzar, and
> the message was true and one of great conflict. And he un-
> derstood the message and had understanding of the vision.
> In those days I, Daniel, was mourning three full weeks. I
> ate no tasty food, no meat or wine entered my mouth, nor did
> I anoint myself at all until three whole weeks were fulfilled.
>
> Daniel 10:1–3

What is the difference between the paranormal and supernatural encounters?

Paranormal events are phenomena such as telekinesis, clair-voyance, and astral projection that are beyond the scope of scientific understanding. The source of these events is the kingdom of darkness. Paranormal events are supernatural encounters, but are not from God. This is why encounters must be interpreted through Scripture to determine their source. In fact, as I said in chapter 4, all spiritual activities must either be validated or rejected based on an accurate interpretation of Scripture. God never violates His Word.

Encounters that do not agree with Scripture must be rejected. You must ask, *Does this encounter glorify God?*

I have never had an encounter. How can I change this?

All believers have experienced supernatural encounters, beginning with encountering Jesus, our Redeemer. If you have experienced healing, this was a healing encounter. The problem can be that focusing on the more visible encounters can lead to missing other types of encounters. Encounters are not a doctrine, and they don't redeem people. Jesus does. Focus on maintaining the altar of prayer and worship in your life, and God-encounters will come. Ask the Lord for an encounter, and He will come.

TEN

Testimonies about Encounters

I am including here several God-encounter testimonies that were submitted to me by credible people whom I know. I have also included two additional encounters that I experienced myself. You will note that each encounter is different, yet they share the commonality of drawing the individual who experienced them closer to the Lord. You will also notice varying degrees of conversation and displays of glory in each encounter. As I have said throughout this book, such God-encounters give us conviction and strengthen our faith.

Testimony of Eleanor Roehl, an apostolic leader from Alaska

As Paul Keith lightly laid hands on me, I felt something go through me and it felt as if it punched me in the gut. It felt like 100 volts of electricity going into my body, and immediately my spirit started shooting through realms, or I should say the heavens. I could feel when I shot through the first realm, and then the second realm, or second heaven. The third heavenly place was a place of absolute fire and the fear of the Lord. As I got to this place, it was as if I was gasping for air because the fire was so hot.

I began to open my eyes, and I saw Jesus come with a book between two of His fingers. He said, *Take and eat My Word, for it will be sweet in your mouth and bitter in your belly.* He said, *I will open up the eyes of your understanding to look into My Word in a new way.*

As He said those things, it was as though He began to teach me. In the few seconds that He was with me, He began unfolding His Word to me in a new way. Then He began to remind me of an encounter I had in 2003. Again, I began gasping for air. There was so much fire and fear of the Lord. I could feel my body shaking violently. I wanted to yell out "*Stop!*" because I thought I was going to die at any minute.

I then began to feel fire in my belly. Jesus said to me, *I am healing the disease in your belly.* I had a disease called H. pylori that causes stomach cancer. A couple of weeks after this experience, I had an appointment to go and get this checked. When Jesus said, *I am healing you of this disease,* I knew it was done.

Then He said, *I'm coming with My Holy Ghost and fire. My Church needs to be baptized afresh in My Holy Ghost fire. My Church knows of My Holy Spirit and is satisfied with speaking in tongues. They are satisfied with just the down payment of My Holy Spirit. There is so much more about My Holy Spirit. My Church needs a fresh baptism of My Holy Ghost and fire. That is how they are going to make it in this new time, this new season and era that the Church is in. For the Church is coming out of a Church mindset into a Kingdom mindset. That is how they will be able to come into this Kingdom mindset and this Kingdom age that we have now stepped into. That will be part of My mandate that I will release here during this time.*

I thought, *There is so much!* Just when I couldn't seem to take it anymore, Jesus said to me, *Open up your spirit eyes.*

As I began to open up my spirit eyes, I just began to look all around me. I saw chariots of fire, and I asked, *Lord, what are these?*

He answered, *These are My angels of fire who will assist the nations of the earth with the war that is at hand and that is ahead.*

Then I began to shake violently. He began to teach me again from the Word, and He told me, *Begin to steward this revelation well. Begin to steward this encounter well. . . .*

For three days, I was in and out of this encounter, with volts of electricity coming into my body. Although I won't share them here, I also received two more amazing encounters.

Testimony of Claudia Henley, a prophetic intercessor from Wisconsin

After moving into my new condo, I couldn't find a chocolate diamond ring I had purchased while on an Alaskan cruise. I asked the Holy Spirit to show me where I had put it.

One morning while I was in the bathroom, one of the lights over the mirror started flashing on and off, as if the lightbulb were going out. But then the flashing would stop and the light would stay on.

This flashing happened over a couple of days, so I finally went downstairs to my supply of lightbulbs to get a new one, and my ring was in the bag, a place I would never have thought to look for it!

After I found the ring, the bathroom light stopped flashing on and off. I knew that this encounter with my flashing bathroom light was an encounter with God answering my prayer.

Testimony of Falma Rufus, a prophetic intercessor from Texas

According to Noah Webster's original 1828 *American Dictionary of the English Language*, one of the definitions of *encounter* is "A meeting face to face, particularly to meet suddenly or unexpectedly." This is what happened between the Lord and me, and between the Lord and my son too, Tracy Turner. We both had a glorious encounter with the Living God.

This testimony begins with Tracy, who was born on July 22, 1969. In 1983, he was diagnosed with bone cancer in one of his knees. He would always complain about his sore knee, because he loved playing basketball. I took him to Children's Medical Center in Dallas, where he was given the diagnosis. I praise the Lord for science and medicine, but more than anything, for our Lord's guidance in all things.

Tracy didn't care for the chemotherapy treatment during his stay at the medical center, even though the staff was more than wonderful. We returned home after he lost his leg due to the cancer and was given a prosthesis so he could walk without crutches. As his mother, I did much praying and crying out to the Lord, and He enabled Tracy to be happy.

This was a season when I leaned heavily on the Word of the Lord, especially Proverbs 3:5 (NASB): "Trust in the LORD with all your heart and do not lean on your own understanding."

Eventually the cancer spread through Tracy's body, to his lungs. I was preparing breakfast for him one Saturday morning when he asked, "How do you get to heaven?"

I led my son in a simple prayer of repentance and accepting Jesus as Lord. I noticed Tracy was a changed child after that, loving God even in all his pain. On one of the doctor visits, he asked the doctor what the results would be, and the young doctor told Tracy that he would die. As we moved through doctor visits and treatments, they just didn't have any way to fight against the cancer. Tracy was given morphine tablets and sent home. There were times when he even refused the pain medication because he didn't like the effects it had.

Then came my encounter: I was continuing to pray and seek the Lord, and one day at my workstation on my job, all of a sudden I was caught up into this glory place. It seemed like a window in heaven, and the presence of the Lord was so glorious! There was light, life, joy, peace, and more. Heaven became the center of all things.

There are no words in any language to describe it, and I knew this was the dwelling place that Jesus, the Father, and the Holy Spirit owned. No conversation was needed because language was unnecessary. As I was coming out of this encounter, one of my work managers came to my desk and walked away in tears simply after seeing me.

I somehow knew that my son had had this same experience. When I came home, I talked with Tracy about it, and he confirmed that he experienced the same encounter with the Lord.

Tracy moved to heaven in April 1986, and we mourned our loss, but also celebrated his life. I am so thankful that our Father God was so generous in allowing heaven to merge with earth in time and space just for Tracy and me.

Testimony of Marty Cassady, a prophetic intercessor from Florida

My friend and I had finished our assignment in Rome and had a few days to spare before traveling back to the United States. We decided to travel to Naples, Italy, and stay with an acquaintance there. Since our hostess was working, we asked her for suggestions on what to do. She asked if we had ever been to Pompeii. Since neither of us had visited that ancient city, we asked the Lord about doing that and got a go-ahead from Him.

Our hostess took us into the city center, and we caught a bus to the train station. She had been very specific about the train stop we should get off at for our visit to Pompeii, so we purchased our tickets, boarded the train, and were on our way. The seating on the train was set up with two seats directly facing two other seats. As the train continued its journey, we realized that soon we were the only women on a train full of men. Since they were speaking in Italian, we couldn't understand the language, but we soon caught the spirit of not only the men, but the evil spirit that had entered our train car. Some of the guys were looking at us and snickering as they spoke to one another.

I silently started crying out to the Lord for help. At the very next train stop, a very tall gentleman entered our train car and sat down directly across from me. He leaned over to me and said, "Take off your watch and your earrings, and put them in your purse."

I was puzzled, to say the least, but there was something about him . . . so I did exactly as he said and removed the watch and earrings. I then noticed how he was dressed, in khaki slacks, a white golf shirt, and a navy blue blazer. He had entered with such authority that the atmosphere in the train car had changed. The young men who had been snickering had stopped, the car had become very silent, and there was a palpable sense of peace.

The tall gentleman leaned over to me once more and asked where my friend and I were going. When I answered him, he then asked me which train stop we were using. When I repeated the stop our hostess had given me, he immediately said, "That's not the right stop. Just follow me off the train, and you will be in the right place!"

There was no other exchange of conversation, and I am estimating that the remainder of the train ride was perhaps another 15 or 20 minutes. We reached our destination and followed the gentleman off the train. He motioned us to the place where we would purchase our tickets to tour Pompeii, and we bought them. When we turned around to thank him, he was gone.

My friend and I looked at one another and knew that we had been directed and protected by an angel sent by God. There have been so many times that I have wondered why I didn't speak with him more during that 15-minute interim. There are so many things in hindsight that I can think of to ask. All I can say is that when the atmosphere of heaven touches down into the human realm, there is a reverence and awe that accompanies it, and questions are not needed or required. My friend and I knew that the fear we had experienced was stilled by a great sense of peace, and we were safe! Our mighty God heard our cry for help, and we were delivered.

Personal Testimony #1, Venner Alston (author)

Several years ago, I was attending a conference. This particular gathering was unlike any I had attended before. The power of God filled every session. Even the children were ministering, laying hands on adults, and incredible power filled the room. At one point, I went back to my hotel room to rest between sessions. I lay across my bed, and suddenly the room was dark. It was as though I were in a movie theater where the curtain opened and the screen lit up. I was looking at myself in this vision. God seemed to be standing behind me. I could hear His voice speaking, and it sounded like thunder.

Every time God's voice thundered, my physical body shook. I didn't know what to make of the events I was watching. I didn't know how to interpret those moments. What I knew is that I was looking at myself in a vision. I was hearing God give me instructions. My body was shaking periodically in response.

My late husband, Bill, had entered the room and noticed my body was shaking. He began to ask me if I was okay, but I could not respond. I could only watch the events unfolding in the vision.

I categorize this particular encounter as a commissioning encounter. The Lord was speaking to me, telling me to prepare my heart to speak for Him. At the time, I had no point of reference concerning encounters. I was just learning about the prophetic and hadn't considered myself a prophet. This was all new to me. Each time God spoke, giving me instructions, my body continued to shake. The thunder of His voice was loud. Even though my eyes were closed as I watched the events unfold on the supernatural screen before me, I could see Bill walk over and sit down beside me in the natural realm and begin to pray.

At the end of the vision, the screen became dark. Up until that moment, I hadn't attempted to rise from my bed. I don't think I could have risen during the vision. I knew I had been captured by the presence of God. When the room became silent, I quickly sat up on the side of the bed. The weight of God was upon me. The power of His glory was flooding my physical being. The reverential fear of God was resting on me as I shook and wept uncontrollably. More than 20 or 30 minutes passed before I could regain my composure. *What was this?* I wondered. *What was God telling me? What do I do with this information?* Since that time, I have often reflected back over this encounter and can see how it has shaped my life and ministry. As I walk with God, He continues to show me how to steward these experiences.

Personal Testimony #2, Venner Alston (author)

I was hosting an event at my church in Milwaukee. Toward the end of the meeting, the visiting prophet asked me to stand and come forward so he could pray for me. As I stood waiting, the Lord spoke to me and said, *Take off your shoes.*

I thought this was odd, but I recognized the voice of God and immediately took my shoes off. When the prophet walked over and laid his hands on me, I immediately dropped to the floor. My face was down toward the carpet. I was in the prayer position, facedown. My body was shaking uncontrollably. Each time I attempted to get up, the shaking would increase.

The next thing I noticed was deep weeping coming from the core of my being. It was a type of travail. Suddenly, in the Spirit I could see a door above me. The door was opened, and I knew that I was in a Revelation 4:1 moment. The Lord spoke to me and said, *You have been given access to this realm. Come through the door.*

There were other things the Lord spoke to me that I won't share just now. But as I continued weeping on the floor, I noticed that still I couldn't get up. I didn't know how much time had passed. After a while, I again attempted to rise. A chair was placed behind me so I could be seated. I opened my eyes, and it appeared as though I was looking into the room from another place. I then noticed that I could not feel my feet on the floor or feel the chair beneath me. The people who were surrounding me seemed two inches tall. The weighty presence of God that was upon me remained for hours. I was speechless for days as I attempted to process the events that had occurred.

Conclusion

The Door Is Open

Call to me and I will answer you and tell you great and unsearchable things you do not know.

Jeremiah 33:3 NIV

The door of supernatural encounters is open. The invitation has been given, and you have been granted access. God longs to share amazing secrets with you. I encourage you to cultivate faith to believe and recognize the encounters God is bringing to you. Ask Him for encounters. Keep in mind the truth that if you are a believer, you have already had at least one supernatural encounter. You have encountered Jesus, our Redeemer. This was the beginning of your encounters. Without encountering the Living Savior, you wouldn't have a conviction of His redemptive work at the cross. We have eternal life through Jesus.

If you operate in the gifts of the Spirit, you have also had an encounter with the Holy Spirit, who speaks to you, revealing truth. There are encounter moments when the Holy Spirit reveals something to you that you did not know.

If you are a serious student of the Bible, chances are you have had an encounter in the Word of God. The Lord is meeting you in the pages of your Bible to show you things about His plans for you and for the nations of the earth.

If you have developed a pattern of prayer and worship, you have probably experienced encounters in those times as well.

This book is designed to encourage you to see beyond the everyday earthly realm, into the realm of the supernatural. God has things He wants to show you. He has a purpose in initiating encounters with you—so that you can know Him deeply, believe that He wants to reveal Himself and His ways to you, and expect that He will fill your times of prayer with His amazing presence.

Listen more deeply. Perhaps God is speaking something to you that you haven't yet heard. Maybe like Elijah, you are looking for Him in the strong wind, but He isn't there. Rather, He is in the still, small voice, as Elijah discovered when God told him to go stand on the mountain before Him:

> And, behold, the LORD passed by, and a great and strong wind split the mountains and broke in pieces the rocks before the LORD, but the LORD was not in the wind. And after the wind, an earthquake came, but the LORD was not in the earthquake. And after the earthquake, a fire came, but the LORD was not in the fire, and after the fire, a still, small voice.
>
> 1 Kings 19:11–12

As you learn to pursue the presence of the Lord, you will find Him. I encourage you to desire Him more than anything else.

I believe we are on the threshold of a supernatural explosion in the Body of Christ. Prayer precedes miracles. The intercessors are praying for miracles, signs, and wonders to return to the Body of Christ. These are encounters. Another way to see this is as the manifesto of heaven overtaking the manifesto of darkness. The Kingdom of heaven will be manifested in the earth. Bishop Bill Hamon writes,

- The Day of the Saints will bring the revelation and activation of every Saint into supernatural manifestations.
- Its finalization will cause the glory of the Lord to fill the earth as waters cover the sea.
- It will bring the revelation of God's progressive and ultimate purpose for His Saints, the Church. . . .
- The greatest harvest of souls ever recorded in Church history will occur during the Day of the Saints.
- Jesus is excited about this coming Day when He will be fully glorified in His Saints.[1]

I encourage you to pursue God and ask for encounters. Interpret the incredible messages He is sending you. Encounters will strengthen your conviction concerning the reality of God and His plans for you. "Jesus Christ is the same yesterday, and today, and forever" (Hebrews 13:8). Spend time in God's presence, and watch Him come! Don't miss your divinely appointed moments. God-encounters are for everyone.

Acknowledgments

I would like to acknowledge the efforts of Kim Bangs, editorial director at Chosen Books, who had vision for this project. Thank you for encouraging me to write such an important book and for praying for me throughout the project.

Notes

Introduction The Invitation

1. *Merriam-Webster Dictionary*, s.v. "manifesto," accessed April 28, 2023, https://www.merriam-webster.com/dictionary/manifesto.

Chapter 1 Understanding Encounters

1. Blue Letter Bible, s.v. "kāḇôḏ" (Strong's H3519), accessed April 28, 2023, https://www.blueletterbible.org/lexicon/h3519/kjv/wlc/0-1/.

2. Barbie Breathitt, *A to Z Dream Symbology Dictionary* (Lake Dallas, Tex.: Barbie Breathitt Enterprises Inc., 2017), 192.

Chapter 2 Living Supernaturally Natural

1. Adam Clarke, *Clarke's Commentary: Matthew–Revelation* (Nashville: Abingdon, 1977), 200.

2. Some of the spirit, soul, and body descriptions in this chapter are drawn from my book *Next-Level Believers* (Chosen, 2022), which you will find helpful to read if you haven't yet done so.

3. Venner J. Alston, *Next-Level Believers: Advanced Strategies for Godly Kingdom Influence* (Minneapolis: Chosen Books, 2022), 33–34.

4. Kenneth Hagin, *Man On Three Dimensions: Volume 1 of the Spirit, Soul, and Body Series* (Broken Arrow, Okla.: Kenneth Hagin Ministries, 1973), 8.

5. Alston, *Next-Level Believers*, 34.

6. Alston, *Next-Level Believers*, 34.

7. W. E. Vine, *Vine's Expository Dictionary of Biblical Words*, eds. Merrill Unger and William White (Nashville: Thomas Nelson, 1985, 1981), 169.

8. Clarke, *Clarke's Commentary: Matthew–Revelation*, 95.

9. Alston, *Next-Level Believers*, 34–35.

10. Alston, *Next-Level Believers*, 35–36.

Chapter 3 The Supernatural Advantage

1. Blue Letter Bible, s.v. "'āḏām" (Strong's H120), accessed April 28, 2023, https://www.blueletterbible.org/lexicon/h120/kjv/wlc/0-1/.

Chapter 4 Legal versus Illegal Encounters

1. Myles Munroe, *Rediscovering the Kingdom: Ancient Hope for Our 21st Century World* (Shippensburg, Pa.: Destiny Image, 2004), 63.

2. Monroe, *Rediscovering the Kingdom*, 64–67.

3. Venner J. Alston, *Next-Level Believers: Advanced Strategies for Godly Kingdom Influence* (Minneapolis: Chosen Books, 2022), 37.

4. Wikipedia, s.v. "manifesto," last modified January 1, 2023, https://en.wikipedia.org/wiki/Manifesto/.

5. Geoff McDonald, "Famous Manifestos—Our Top Ten," February 27, 2011, https://geoffmcdonald.com/famous-manifestos/.

6. Blue Letter Bible, s.v. "'ĕlōhîm" (Strong's H430), accessed April 28, 2023, https://www.blueletterbible.org/lexicon/h430/kjv/wlc/0-1/.

7. For more on the structure of the heavens, see my book *Next-Level Spiritual Warfare: Advanced Strategies for Defeating the Enemy* (Chosen, 2019), particularly pages 40–41.

8. *Merriam-Webster Dictionary*, s.v. "occult," accessed April 28, 2023, https://www.merriam-webster.com/dictionary/occult.

9. *Statista*, "Market Size of the Psychic Services Industry in the U.S. 2011–2022," February 3, 2023, https://www.statista.com/statistics/1224176/psychic-services-market-size-us/.

10. Dictionary.com, s.v. "good vibes," accessed April 28, 2023, https://www.dictionary.com/e/slang/good-vibes/.

11. *CBN News*, "Ex-Psychic Warns of Yoga: 'You're Opening Demonic Doors,'" *Charisma*, December 16, 2022, https://charismamag.com/spiritled-living/faith/ex-psychic-warns-of-yoga-youre-opening-demonic-doors/.

12. Leland Ryken, James C. Wilhoit, and Tremper Longman III, eds., *Dictionary of Bible Imagery* (Downers Grove, Ill.: InterVarsity, 1998), 207.

13. W. E. Vine, *Vine's Expository Dictionary of Biblical Words*, eds. Merrill Unger and William White (Nashville: Thomas Nelson, 1985, 1981), 328.

14. For more on this, see the entry from *Vine's Expository Dictionary of Biblical Words* cited in note 13.

Chapter 5 Portals, Gates, and Doors

1. Dr. Candice Smithyman, "The Access Points You Need for Entry Into Heavenly Portals," *Charisma*, February 3, 2022, https://charismamag .com/spiritled-living/supernaturaldreams/the-access-points-you-need-for -entry-into-heavenly-portals/.

2. W. E. Vine, *Vine's Expository Dictionary of Biblical Words*, eds. Merrill Unger and William White (Nashville: Thomas Nelson, 1985, 1981), 26.

3. Venner J. Alston, *Next-Level Believers: Advanced Strategies for Godly Kingdom Influence* (Minneapolis: Chosen Books, 2022), 68–69.

4. Alston, *Next-Level Believers*, 69–71.

5. Smithyman, "Access Points."

6. Leland Ryken, James C. Wilhoit, and Tremper Longman III, eds., *Dictionary of Bible Imagery* (Downers Grove, Ill.: InterVarsity, 1998), 215.

7. Adam Clarke, *Clarke's Commentary: Matthew-Revelation* (Nashville: Abingdon, 1977), 985.

8. Venner J. Alston, *Breakthrough Prayers, Decrees and Confessions: Overcoming Demonic Resistance through Warfare Prayer* (Mequon, Wis.: VJ Alston International Ministries, 2019), 44.

9. Adapted from Alston, *Breakthrough Prayers, Decrees and Confessions*, 40.

Chapter 6 Presence Driven

1. Tommy Tenney, *The God Chasers: My Soul Follows Hard after Thee* (Shippensburg, Pa.: Destiny Image, 1998), Kindle edition, 37 of 159.

2. Leland Ryken, James C. Wilhoit, and Tremper Longman III, eds., *Dictionary of Bible Imagery* (Downers Grove, Ill.: InterVarsity, 1998), 231.

3. W. E. Vine, *Vine's Expository Dictionary of Biblical Words*, eds. Merrill Unger and William White (Nashville: Thomas Nelson, 1985, 1981), 233.

4. Venner Alston, *Next-Level Believers: Advanced Strategies for Godly Kingdom Influence* (Minneapolis: Chosen Books, 2022), 18.

5. Adapted from Venner J. Alston, *Breakthrough Prayers, Decrees and Confessions: Overcoming Demonic Resistance through Warfare Prayer* (Mequon, Wis.: VJ Alston International Ministries, 2019), 24.

Chapter 7 Fire on the Altar

1. Chuck D. Pierce and Alemu Beeftu, *Rekindle the Altar Fire: Making a Place for God's Presence* (Minneapolis: Chosen Books, 2020), Kindle edition, 45 of 209.

2. Pierce and Beeftu, *Rekindle the Altar Fire*, 92 of 209.

3. Pierce and Beeftu, *Rekindle the Altar Fire*, 92 of 209.

4. For more on this, see Leland Ryken, James C. Wilhoit, and Tremper Longman III, eds., *Dictionary of Biblical Imagery* (Downers Grove, Ill.: InterVarsity, 1998), 20.

5. Pierce and Beeftu, *Rekindle the Altar Fire*, 22 of 209.

6. Ryken, Wilhoit, and Longman, *Dictionary of Biblical Imagery*, 21.

7. Kevin J. Conner, *The Temple of Solomon: The Glory of God as Displayed through the Temple* (Portland, Ore.: City Bible Publishing, 1988), 55.

8. Conner, *Temple of Solomon*, 55.

9. Pierce and Beeftu, *Rekindle the Altar Fire*, 26 of 209.

10. Paula Price, *The Prophet's Dictionary: The Ultimate Guide to Supernatural Wisdom* (Tulsa: Flaming Vision Publications, 1999), 218.

Chapter 8 Sustaining Encounters

1. Paula Price, *The Prophet's Dictionary: The Ultimate Guide to Supernatural Wisdom* (Tulsa: Flaming Vision Publications, 1999), 574.

2. Barbie Breathitt, *Angels in God's Kingdom* (Lake Dallas, Tex.: Barbie Breathitt Enterprises Inc., 2017), 2.

Conclusion The Door Is Open

1. Dr. Bill Hamon, *The Day of the Saints: Equipping Believers for their Revolutionary Role In Ministry* (Shippensburg, Pa.: Destiny Image, 2002), Kindle edition, 14 of 433.

Dr. Venner J. Alston travels internationally to communicate hope and offer Kingdom solutions for individual and societal issues. She is a commissioned apostle, gifted author, teacher, and speaker.

In addition to earning a doctoral degree in Urban Education from the University of Wisconsin-Milwaukee, Dr. Alston is certified as a life coach with several organizations, including the John Maxwell Group. She is a member of the International Coaching Federation (ICF) and also holds a certification in Women in Leadership and Psychology of Leadership from Cornell University.

Dr. Alston is founder and apostle of Global Outreach Ministries and Training Center, and The Exceptional Woman mentoring and ministry group. She hosts *Destiny Moments with Dr. Venner Alston* on Sid Roth's It's Supernatural Network. Her podcast, *Destiny Moments with Dr. Venner Alston*, airs weekly. She is also aligned with Kingdom Harvest Alliance Inc., led by Apostle Chuck Pierce.

Dr. Alston lives in Milwaukee, Wisconsin, and is the author of these other books:

Next-Level Believers: Advanced Strategies for Godly Kingdom Influence (Chosen, 2022)

Image Bearer: Restoring the Power and Truth of the Image of God within You (VJ Alston International Ministries, 2020)

Next-Level Spiritual Warfare: Advanced Strategies for Defeating the Enemy (Chosen, 2019)

Breakthrough Prayers, Decrees and Confessions: Overcoming Demonic Resistance through Warfare Prayer (VJ Alston International Ministries, 2019).

For more information on Dr. Alston and her ministry, visit

- @iamdrvjalston
- @iamdrvjalston2
- @iamdrvjalston
- @iamdrvjalston
- @Dr. VJ Alston TV

www.drvjalston.org